MW01104722

Handwritten inscription: Nov. 2, 2005 — Dr. Ch... — years of good dental care — Grove Armstrong — Psalms 84:10-12

The *Kingdom* that is
TRANSFORMING
the World

Grove Armstrong

TATE PUBLISHING, LLC

"The Kingdom That Is Transforming The World" by Grove Armstrong

This book is designed to provide accurate and authoritative information with regard to the subject matter covered. This information is given with the understanding that neither the author nor Tate Publishing, LLC is engaged in rendering legal, professional advice. Since the details of your situation are fact dependent, you should additionally seek the services of a competent professional.

ISBN: 1–5988603–4-8

TO

My Friends and Family,
who from my earliest recollections
have enriched my life.

ACKNOWLEDGEMENTS

The seed for this book was planted in my mind in the early 1990s while I studied the Scriptures, working on sermons for the Christmas season. Bob Gordon, my friend and parishioner, had such a positive response to a sermon on the "Everlasting Increase and the Wonderful Benefits of Messiah's Kingdom" that it inspired me to think more about it. I began to talk about the thesis with others and received mixed reviews. Some thought that perhaps I was correct, but others were not persuaded. To those *un-persuaded* ones, I owe a great debt of gratitude. It was those good folk, and there were several, who inspired my seven years of research to see (1) if these truly are the best times in history, and (2) if Jesus is really the reason they are so wonderful. The story that emerged from my study is so wonderful that I want to tell it.

There is a special friend in my life, my high school English teacher, Mrs. Jean Munger Rich to whom I owe a great deal of gratitude. Upon learning of my intention to write this book, she continually checked with me to see how it was coming. Finally, she wrote me a letter saying, "It is time to start writing. I want 100 pages by Christmas." It was the right word at the right time from the right person. I began writing and two years later completed the manuscript.

To the several former teachers who read the earliest portions of the manuscript and made helpful suggestions, encouraging me to continue, I am also indebted. They are the Rev. and Mrs. Coral R. Ide, B.A., B.D., Mr. Darrel Thompson, Ed.M., Mr. Gary Butler, M.A., Dr. Allan Seimers Ed.D., and Mr. Robert Gordon M.A., Ed.M.

To Dr. DuWayne Howell Ed.D. and his wife, Judy Howell Ed.M., and to Dr. Charles E. Bollinger Ed.D., I owe an immense debt of gratitude for their thorough study of the completed manuscript and their invaluable instructions and suggestions for editing the manuscript. Without their instruction and counsel, this book would never have been accepted by any publisher.

To author Susan Wereska, Ed.M, I owe many thanks for giving me the information that enabled me to move the completed manuscript from my computer to the desk of an interested publisher. I had no idea how to present or market my manuscript. She kindly, patiently, and enthusiastically spent much time going into detail as to how to do it, answering many e-mails whenever I needed guidance. She read and corrected my first marketing efforts and gave me strong motivation to work until I found a publisher saying, "The church needs to hear this encouraging message."

My youngest son salvaged the book when my computer crashed and all the backups proved useless. I thought the work of several years was gone, but Carl searched the Internet and found a company that would try to recover the manuscript for me. Thank God, they successfully recovered the entire manuscript including all my research information and bibliography, saving me from what would have been a very painful loss.

My oldest son, Clifton M.M, M.A., insisted that I slash every unnecessary, redundant, repetitive and useless word and paragraph from the manuscript. He has undeniably and unquestionably made it better. I appreciated his painful over-the-shoulder examination of my first feeble attempt at word slashing. It was humiliating, but it started me on a serious venture to improve the book by shortening it. Hopefully, I succeeded. Thanks, Professor.

Our daughter, Betty Anne Hotham, was a tremendous help—receiving for me the letters from publishing houses, reading, and forwarding those I needed to see while we traveled around the country. I also appreciate her significant help searching out information on the Internet when either I did not have that service available to me or was not sufficiently proficient to find out the information myself.

I am honored and grateful to Dr. Wesley E. Vanderhoof, Ph.D., retired Chairman of the Division of Religion and Humanities and Professor of Biblical Literature at Roberts Wesleyan College, Rochester, NY, and to Dr. G. Herbert Livingston, Ph.D. retired Professor of Old Testament and Chair of the Division of Biblical Studies at Asbury Theological Seminary, Wilmore, KY, for writing forewords for my book.

And last, but by no means least, I thank my wonderful wife, Charity Peaton Armstrong—herself an experienced teacher, writer, and proofreader—for her unfailing enthusiasm for this work, her helpful suggestions, meticulous proofreading, and tireless editing. Without her help and encouragement, this book would never have become a reality.

TABLE OF CONTENTS

FOREWORD TO PART I

The early chapters of the Book of Acts show the apostles both elated and confused at the resurrection and appearances of Jesus. Told to "wait for the promise of the Father," they stayed in Jerusalem, united in purpose, devoted to prayer, and committed to waiting for whatever it was that God had in store for them. At the same time, they were under a mandate to " …go into all the world and preach the gospel to every creature." So there they were, waiting to begin a mission they could not have fully understood, but needing the promised power before they could launch it.

That was then, about 2000 years ago. As the Book of Acts tells us, the apostles did successfully launch the mission, first to Jerusalem, then to Judea, further outward to Galilee and Samaria, and beyond. The story of Acts advances the "good news" all the way to Rome. Along the way, it impacted Cyprus, Asia Minor, Greece, Dalmatia, Crete, and Macedonia. Hundreds, even thousands, became believers, including some of the household of Caesar (Philippians 4:22). Luke traces that history until sometime in the mid- to late-sixties. Later writings, outside of the New Testament, reveal to us that within a few hundred years the church had extended to Egypt, North Africa, India, and Syria. Of course, historians have chronicled the spread of the Christian faith from those days until the present.

To summarize that history is not necessary. It is important, however, to try to answer the question: How are we doing in the 21st century toward the fulfillment of the Great Commission? That is the purpose of this book. Using Isaiah 9 as a starting point, the author offers up an optimistic picture for our consideration. "The people who walked in darkness have seen a great light; those who dwelt in a land of deep darkness, on them has light shined…They rejoice before thee as with joy at the harvest, as men rejoice when they divide the spoil. For the yoke of his burden, and the staff for his shoulder, the rod of his oppressor, thou hast broken as on the day of Midian. "...For unto us a child is born, to us a son is given; and the government will be upon his shoulder ...Of the increase of his government and of peace there will be no end...with justice and with righteousness from this time forth and forevermore. The zeal of the Lord of hosts will do this." (Isaiah 9:2-3,6-7 RSV)

Declaring that the Christian Gospel has always had a significant, positive impact upon societies where it has been embraced. The author wonders why evangelicals express little optimism about the future of the church and the world in which and to which it proclaims that Gospel. While the headlines scream terror, war, and catastrophe, giving us justifiable reason to hang our heads and even to wonder if the cause of righteousness and peace is winning the field, the Christian Church is putting forth great effort to advance the rule of God around the world, and it is having great success improving the quality of life on the planet. The author states his belief in the vision of Isaiah, who saw a better future and affirmed that God's universal rule would increase and that it would never come to an end or be overcome. Think about that. If it is true that no matter how strong evil appears and no matter how powerfully the redemption of God's creation is resisted, and there will be no end to the increase of the Son's government, then we may confidently envision the coming of a new day. We can be assured that the gospel will have a growing impact upon earth's societies, an impact that is both uplifting and redeeming.

From our present perspective, we can see that Isaiah's words were truly spoken. The Gospel, upon which the rule of Christ is based, has indeed had a tremendously positive sociological and political impact upon human culture. Now we know, of course, evil remains strong within our world.

There is ample evidence that the forces of evil have been and still are hard at work to keep the promised blessings of God's rule from coming to pass. It is certainly true that knowing the truth of the Gospel does not necessarily result in enlightened behavior. We have only to recognize that the country that gave birth to the Reformation also engendered the Third Reich. We recognize, too, the nation with probably the greatest Christian influence struggles with high crime rates, serious drug abuse, high divorce rates, rampant pornography, and extensive human abuse, and that it tolerates abortion and is unclear about the definition of marriage. Yet the author maintains, society is being redeemed and blessed through Christ, even as God promised Abraham in Genesis 12:3; " ... And the entire world will be blessed because of you." (The Living Bible) In other words, not only will individuals be redeemed, but the societies in which the Gospel is embraced will also be refashioned. The coming of Jesus changed forever the character of life in the world and continues to alter positively the course of life on the planet. Thus the author contends, in nations where the Gospel has gone and been accepted, the conditions of human life have improved.

The New Testament suggests (Ephesians 1, for example) that God intended the Church to be the true agent of change in the world. History has shown that to be the case. It continues to be a powerful change agent, because Jesus' teachings offered answers to the basic human questions. The newly-born Church soon grasped the power of those teachings and of the life, death, and resurrection of the Master to change the whole world. Therefore, those early believers began to rethink Jesus' ultimate purpose in coming. They began to catch the prophets' visions of the world as the object of God's love. It began to dawn upon them that the kingdom of God, of which Jesus spoke, was to change the world for the better.

The church continues to take seriously the challenge to improve the world by taking the gospel everywhere.

"From Greenland's icy mountains,
From India's coral strand;
Where Afric's sunny fountains
Roll down their golden sand;
From many an ancient river,
From many a palmy plain,
They call us to deliver
Their land from error's chain."
(Reginald Heber, 1819)[1]

And across the world God is moving to improve the status of his creatures, the objects of divine love. A few years ago, many of us Christians were singing of the Spirit's moving all over the world and revealing God's glory everywhere. At the time, even those who were not sure it was true sang hopefully. However, the evidence suggests that it is true. The Spirit **is** moving all over the world. We need to open our eyes and see God at work, even as he promised: "...For a law will go forth from me, and my justice for a light to the peoples. My deliverance draws near speedily, my salvation has gone forth, and my arms will rule the peoples; the coastlands wait for me, and for my arm they hope." (Isaiah 51:4–5 RSV) And in the following chapter of Isaiah, God's saving action is affirmed with these words, "The Lord has bared his holy arm before the eyes of all the actions; and all the ends of the earth shall see the salvation of our God." (Isaiah 52:10 RSV)

Chapter 6 of Acts tells us that the apostles, although they were determined to teach and preach, saw the human need around them and took steps to meet that need. In the situation recorded in Acts 6, they appointed deacons to minister to the needs of the Hellenistic (Greek-speaking), Jewish widows who were being neglected in the regular distribution of provisions. Since that time, the Christian church has set itself to give the cup of cold water in Jesus' name. All over the world, wherever the gospel has gone, the followers of Jesus have been meeting human need, and in the process, they have been changing lives and societies for the better. The widespread missionary movement of the last two hundred years has not only carried the gospel, but it has brought practical relief around the world to people in need, drastically improving the quality of life in the nonwestern world. Jesus said, "I came that they may have life, and have it abundantly." (John 10:10 RSV) A look at the numbers will show that the efforts of the church around the world continue at an intense pace. The words of Paul to the Colossians, many years ago, seem appropriate in our day: "All over the world this gospel is bearing fruit and growing." (Colossians 1:6 RSV)

Within the last fifty years, nearly ninety new missionary organizations have sprung up, guided by the Great Commission. The author cites many examples of these new ministries that have been developed in the last half century in response to Jesus' charge to take the gospel to the world. Many more might be mentioned to further document that the church of Jesus Christ is alive and well across the face of the planet. In addition, there are denominational mission organizations that are serving the needy in Jesus' name as they share the good news of the gospel. If the disciples of John the Baptist were to come into our midst with their question: Is Jesus the one, or should we be waiting for another? We could answer as Jesus answered, "Go tell John what you have seen and heard; the blind receive their sight, the lame walk, lepers are cleansed, and the deaf hear, the dead are raised up, the poor have the good news preached to them." (Luke 7:22 RSV) In our day, these words of Isaiah are being fulfilled. " ...I am coming to gather all nations and tongues; and they shall come and shall see my glory, and I will set a sign among them. And from them I will send survivors to the nations…, to the coastlands afar off, that have not heard my fame or seen my glory; and they shall declare my glory among the nations." (Isaiah 66:18,19 RSV)

Of course, most of us are realists. We see the great trouble that our world is experiencing, and we are tempted to despair. Insurgents and terrorists seem determined to disrupt God's plans. Even legitimate governments have taken a stand against Christianity by declaring it an outlaw religion. Yet God's Spirit is moving. As we move closer and closer to the end, the activity of the evil one will increase, and the devil and his forces will intensify their attacks upon the people of earth. Although we are warned of this increase in demonic activity in the last days, we can be assured that God intends to lay all the kingdoms of the earth at Jesus' feet. Even in countries where Christianity is forbidden, the efforts of the church through its missionaries are bearing fruit. Following the tsunami that devastated much of Southeast Asia in 2004, Indonesia issued a warning that, while humanitarian relief efforts are welcome, the Christian gospel is not, and that those who attempt to evangelize in this Muslim nation in the name of tsunami relief will be sent home. Of course, much of that relief is being sponsored by Christian organizations. It remains to be seen how this catastrophe may prove to be yet another opportunity for God's Spirit to work.

The church of Jesus Christ is alive and well. Never before in history has it been so active in both carrying the gospel to the ends of the earth and endeavoring to ameliorate the suffering that evil inflicts. There are more missionaries than ever before, and Christians contribute billions of dollars yearly to spread the gospel and to relieve human misery. We may say with confidence, then, the church continues to have a marvelous redeeming impact upon society. The promise to Abraham, the world would be blessed by his heir, is undeniably true, in spite of all the hatred and deception of the enemy. Wherever the gospel has gone, the benefits of the kingdom, both spiritual and material, have followed. Men and women are changed, and they in turn, change their society for the better. It is happening according to a divine plan; it is happening in our time; it is happening all over the world. "And of the increase of his government there shall be no end."

The Reverend, Mr. Armstrong was active as a minister for many years, and as a preacher, he has carefully studied the Scriptures. This book arises out of his perception that many evangelicals are pessimistic about where God is permitting the world to drift. On the contrary, he believes that the Bible paints a different picture, a picture of hope for the world, and he believes that the Spirit has used the life, teachings, and death and Resurrection of Jesus to improve life among God's creatures wherever faith is allowed to take root and grow, all over the world.

Wesley E. Vanderhoof, Ph.D
North Chili, New York

FOREWORD TO PART II

Armstrong uses this section of his book to present two significant verses from the Old Testament and two from the New Testament to support his thesis that the Salvation Plan of the Almighty God will triumph over evil. Taking his cue from these verses, Armstrong affirms that Satan and his cohorts have been and will continue to be fearfully strong in this world, but God is ever in ultimate control and conquers evil by His own methods. Always there will be a fierce contest between God and Satan. The climatic moment was the death and resurrection of Jesus Christ and the ultimate moment with be the Second Coming of Christ. Armstrong starts with two passages: Isaiah 9:7 and Daniel 2:31–35, 44–45. Isaiah is brief and positive, "Of the increase of His government and peace there will be no end." (NKJV). The Messiah will be the ultimate Victor. This affirmation is the foundation for optimism. In the Book Daniel, the mighty Nebuchadnezzar had seen an image during a dream and only Daniel could interpret it. In brief, God's kingdom would destroy all other kingdoms and His alone shall stand forever. Daniel declared the interpretation was sure.

In the Gospels, (Matthew 13:31–32, and parallels) Jesus used the tiny mustard seed, and yeast (Matthew 13:33) to illustrate how he would overcome Satan; The point is that Jesus does not need great armies to win the day.

Armstrong then brings together an array of Scriptures from Gen 9:11 through the Psalter to show that realism about evil but optimism about Redemptive Grace is prevalent in the ancient records, especially those related to King David. Expositions of the verses, passages and events cited are helpful and should be easily understood. Sentences are well constructed and the vocabulary can be grasped easily by the average reader.

Armstrong returns to the writings of prophet by providing an excellent exposition of the entire book of Isaiah to support the affirmation in 9:7. The portions selected from Ezekiel, Daniel, Joel, Micah and Zechariah are explained adequately. These prophets are solidly on the side of Armstrong's thesis.

Armstrong begins his discussion of the New Testament with the petition in the Lord's Prayer (Matthew 6:10) "Your kingdom come, Your will be done, On earth as it is in heaven." Besides forgiveness, the plea is for a better society. This emphasis is backed by three other statements in Matthew and correlated with Isaiah 9:7 and Ephesians 1:22.

The Acts of the Apostles provides narrative of how the Holy Spirit empowers the disciples to change Jerusalem and other cities and nations gradually through revival and faithful witnessing. Armstrong concludes that his discussion of New Testament content supports his thesis that the superior work of the Holy Spirit is primary to the New Testament. Though 2 Timothy 3:1–9 is a true description of a wicked society, Paul's testimony is also true, "The Lord delivered me," 2 Timothy 3:11. And Paul's vision of the positive power of the Scripture will mature faithful Christians so each is "complete, thoroughly equipped for every good work". (2 Tim 3:16–17)

Armstrong's book is an excellent study of an important theme in the Scriptures. We trust every reader of this volume will take the admonitions of the author to heart and become an effective transformer of individuals and society as a whole.

G. Herbert Livingston Ph.D
Wilmore, Kentucky

PREFACE

The Christian Gospel is the most positive, encouraging, redeeming, and transforming witness the world has ever heard. Christians, therefore, ought to be the most positive, hopeful, excited people on earth. However, it does not appear to be so. There is a great paradox within the evangelical church. On the one hand, it is putting forth tremendous effort and making incredible advances all over the world, but on the other hand, there is little optimism and much pessimism among Christians about conditions in the world. Even the future of the church is, for many, a matter of anxiety. The church is turning the world right side up with its evangelistic message and benevolent deeds, yet it is spreading among itself a message of pessimism. A young father recently expressed the sentiment to me that with so much evil in the world, he wasn't interested in bringing other children into the world.

Given the aggressive, worldwide proclamation of the powerful transforming message of the Gospel, it seems strange that so many declare, "We have moved beyond the Christian era." They are actually saying, "Evil is winning and Satan is overcoming the Lord and his church. Our situation is hopeless. It is time for the Lord to come and take his believing children off to a better land where evil can no longer touch or threaten them."

These pessimistic ideas do not harmonize with Jesus who said, "All authority in heaven and on earth has been given to me. Therefore go and make disciples of all nations." (Matthew 28:18–19) According to Jesus, the Sadducees did not believe in the Resurrection because they did "not know the Scriptures or the power of God" (Matthew 22:29). That may explain why there is so much pessimism about the future of the church and the world in the modern church. We are too impressed by the media's presentation of our times and too little impressed with the Scriptures and the dynamic power of God.

Hundreds of years ago, the Holy Spirit spoke through the Prophet Isaiah of the birth of the Christ, promising that "Of the increase of his government and peace there will be no end." (Isaiah 9:7) Notice, the Holy Spirit says there will be "no end to the increase." No matter how evil the world was into which the King was born, no matter how powerfully and stubbornly evil resists, no matter how imperfect or ineffective or even uncommitted and often disobedient Christ's subjects are, Scripture says that Christ's kingdom will increase continually. The Spirit promises that "The zeal of the Lord of Hosts will accomplish this." (Isaiah 9:7) The continual increase of the kingdom of God in this world will not depend on man's abilities or enthusiasm, but upon God's. Neither will men or devils be able to stop its increase and impact.

This book is an attempt to bring two things to the attention of the church. (1) There will be no end to the INCREASE of Christ's kingdom in this world, nor to its positive, uplifting, redeeming IMPACT upon the societies of this world, until Christ does, indeed, return. (2) Jesus is the reason for the almost indescribable difference between the world into which Christ was born and our world today.

The impact of Christ's kingdom on this present world will continue to be so profound as to vindicate the love of God for man in placing him on this planet. It gives glory to the Creator for the amazing wonders that he placed in this world. Christ's kingdom will totally discredit Satan for all the evil that he implied against the Creator when he lied to our original parents in the Garden of Eden.

As contrary as this truth is to the depressing opinion expressed so often today in the pulpits of the world, this concept has literally been forced upon me by the Scriptures. Furthermore, the Holy Spirit has demonstrated how, throughout history, Jesus has been transforming the societies of our world through his church. The wonderful truth is that he continues to change our world for the better and the future looks even brighter.

Chapter 1 of Part I fleshes out these insights so the reader will know the full ramifications of these significant truths. Chapter 2 describes, as much as words can, the world into which Jesus came. Chapter 3 presents and demonstrates, from history, a profound truth of which most people, Christians and nonbelievers alike, are totally unaware. This chapter shows conclusively that the difference between living conditions in the pre-Christian world and the wonderful life we enjoy today is simply Jesus the Christ. Jesus, the Lord of history, present in his church/kingdom, has wrought this incredible change. Chapter 4 demonstrates that Jesus is not finished with his gracious healing and transforming ministry to our hurting world. The reader will see here just how active, robust, and rapidly expanding is his kingdom today, in spite of tremendous worldwide opposition.

The Bible, the inspired Word of God, is the bedrock of all Christian doctrine. No teaching should be believed or expounded if it is not clearly taught in the Bible. Therefore, Part II lays out the scriptural support for the truth presented in this book. From Genesis through the New Testament, scriptural passages are noted that imply or teach clearly the continuing growth and victory of the kingdom of God and its prophesied, powerfully redeeming impact upon the civilizations and societies of this world. These Scriptures demonstrate that the Bible is consistent in its optimistic outlook for the future. After considering this information, the reader can understand that the incredible improvement in the quality of life that Jesus has brought to this world is the actual fulfillment of Old Testament prophecies and Jesus' promises. The reader will then have a much more biblical and therefore more hopeful outlook on the future. Wherever his kingdom goes, Jesus continues to improve the quality of life in this world while inspiring a living hope for life in the next.

This little book is sent out into the church with the prayer that it will encourage Christians to consider and rejoice in all the Lord Jesus has already done and all that he is going to do in this world. May it inspire praise to God and a more positive personal outlook and a more powerful prayerful witness to the despairing and hopeless peoples of our world.

Most of the Scriptures quoted in this book have direct reference to the kingdom but some refer to the church. The King of the kingdom is the Lord of the church and the subjects of the kingdom are the members of the church. It is obvious that prophecies about the kingdom are, for the most part, true of the church as well. For instance, when Jesus said, "…I will build my church…" (Matthew 16:18), he was saying essentially the same thing as when he said, "The kingdom of God is like a mustard seed, which a man took and planted in his field. Though it is the smallest of all your seeds, yet when it grows, it is the largest of garden plants and becomes a tree …" (Matthew 13:31–32) There is, therefore, no need in this book to make any distinction between the kingdom of God and the church of the Lord Jesus in their combined impact upon society.

Bishop G. W. Griffith noted the multitude of times the Greek word, *basileia,* translated "kingdom," is used in the Gospels and the number of times the Greek word *ekklesia,* translated "church", is used in the Acts of the Apostles and the remainder of the New Testament. He believed that "This clearly proves that *basileia* is the pre-Pentecost word, while *ekklesia* is the post-Pentecost word."[2]

Because the ideas discussed in this book are such a departure from the prevalent contemporary evangelical opinion that sees only "perilous times coming," the reader may seriously question the truths presented here. Without having read the book, some have already spoken to me their objections. Apparently, it is inconceivable to many Christians that it could possibly be God's will that there be a bright future for the kingdom and the world. Consequently, the book closes with an epilogue in which I will try to answer the questions that have often been expressed to me.

PART I

THE EXPANSION AND IMPACT OF THE KINGDOM OF GOD

*"In the days to come Jacob will take root, Israel will bud
and blossom and fill all the world with fruit." (Isaiah 27:6)*

*And the glory of the LORD will be revealed, and
all mankind together will see it. For the mouth
of the LORD has spoken." (Isaiah 40:5)*

ONE

A New Look At The Kingdom Of God

The ancient prophet, Isaiah, has told us that there
will be no end to the INCREASE of Christ's kingdom in this
world. Speaking of the Messiah, Isaiah promises in Chapter
9, verse 7, "Of the increase of his government and peace
there will be no end." Isaiah also often spoke of the Messiah's kingdom's positive, uplifting, redeeming IMPACT upon
the societies of this world, to the everlasting glory of God.
His words are discussed at length in Part II. These encouraging and exciting prophecies are being fulfilled in wonderful
ways today. The increase and healthful impact of the kingdom of God are gaining momentum as the years roll on.

The eternal characteristics of the kingdom of God
and its ever-living king, Jesus, have always been a major
theme of the church. Yet seldom is any significant emphasis
put upon the ever-increasing aspect of the kingdom, except
that it would eventually reach to all nations. Surprisingly,
little has been made of the transforming effect that the kingdom of God has had upon the societies wherever it has gone

in this world. It is certainly an exaggeration to say that dividing history into two time periods, B.C. and A.D., is about all the recognition given to Jesus for his revolutionary impact. Yet little credit is given to him for the tremendous positive sociological, technical, medical, and political changes that have come about in this world since he came as Teacher, Savior and King.

The wonderfully inspiring truth this book highlights and celebrates is that the Gospel of Jesus is not only going to be carried to the uttermost parts of the earth, but that it will be preached everywhere with great effectiveness. Jesus will powerfully establish his kingdom in all nations and change for the better every place the gospel goes and every society it touches.

When Satan approached Eve in the Garden of Eden, as recorded in Genesis Chapter 3, it seems his main intention was to discredit God—to make God look evil and make himself look good. He implied that God was not her friend and that he himself was. God wanted to keep her from the good life, while Satan wanted her to have it. With Satan's attack upon God's character and intentions in mind, it is this book's contention that our gracious Lord and Creator God is not content just to save his church out of this evil society and take it to another safer and nicer place. Rather, God intends through his church/kingdom to so transform this world's society that his genuine love and all the good things he had planned for his creation will be seen on earth. Satan's blasphemous accusations against God will be revealed as the lies they were. He will be totally discredited before all men. He will be seen for the evil being that he is. God himself says, "For my own sake, for my own sake, I do this. How can I let myself be defamed? I will not yield my glory to another." (Isaiah 48:11)

On the other hand, God's great love and gracious intentions for his created beings will become more and more obvious on earth. Already we see God's unsearchable genius in the amazing things He has put into his creation. The incredible advances in technology and medicine of the past fifty years have only scratched the surface of what God has created and made possible. They give us abundant reason to praise him for all the benefits he daily sends our way. It is awe-inspiring to discover the almost miraculous things that the Lord put into creation that make our lives here comfortable and constructive and pleasure-filled. In the book of Isaiah, God says that He does wonderful things for his people "…so that people may see and know…that the hand of the Lord has done this, that the Holy One of Israel has created it." (Isaiah 41:20)

Since the Fall (Genesis 3), the beautiful world that God created groans under evil's corrupting influence. (Romans 8:22) Until Christ does return, evil will be present in our society and impact multitudes. Nevertheless, those privileged to live in these days are enjoying the beautiful benefits of life in a society that is being powerfully redeemed, transformed, and blessed. We will experience, to an ever-increasing degree, the blessing promised to Abraham through the ministry of his glorious heir. "I will make you into a great nation and I will bless you…All peoples of the earth will be blessed through you." (Genesis 12:3) Jesus, the son of Abraham, is the triumphant Redeemer King who transforms fallen men and civilizations.

Unfortunately today, too little is made of those great promises and way too much is made of one statement in the Bible relative to the condition of the world as time goes on.

"There will be terrible times in the last days. People will be lovers of themselves, lovers of money, boastful, proud, abusive, disobedient to their parents, ungrateful, unholy, without love, unforgiving, slanderous, without self-control, brutal, not lovers of the good, treacherous, rash, conceited, lovers of pleasure rather than lovers of God, having a form of godliness, but denying its power." (2 Timothy 3:1–5)

These words of the Apostle Paul to Timothy seem to be the only lens through which large numbers of Christians see their world. Tragically, many see only that "terrible times" are coming. In fact, many are convinced that terrible times are here now. They read newspapers, watch gruesome events on television, and conclude that Paul's prophetic words have come to pass, and we are definitely in "the last days." Incredibly, someone has come up with the term, "The Post-Christian Era" to describe our times. It is being accepted by many and often proclaimed as a valid definition of our day.

It would be ridiculous to deny that there are terrible things happening in our world, but it seems to have escaped notice that terrible things have always been happening. Life in this world has always been perilous. Didn't the very first baby born into this world kill his own brother? Satan's implied promise of a wonderful, blessed life to those who believed he was their friend did not prove true. The result of our first parents' disobedience has been violence, chaos, havoc, and unimaginable suffering in the world right from the beginning. Didn't Cain embody all the characteristics that Paul said would be prevalent in the last days?

Since that tragic day when Adam and Eve disobeyed God and sin entered our world, times have always been terrible—in fact, much more terrible than they are today. We have read the Bible and failed to notice the terribleness, the ugliness, the violence, the blood, and the pain that was everywhere evident, taken for granted by everyone. When reading the Bible, if one makes an effort to note the living conditions of the people in the Bible, he will see that both the Old and New Testaments picture a society utterly inhumane, murderous, dangerous, sexually promiscuous, and evil beyond comprehension. Furthermore, he will note that suffering and sorrow were the common lot of all men, rich as well as poor. The village into which Jesus was born and the city where he died, regardless of how romantically they are pictured on Christmas cards and children's Sunday school picture cards, were dirty, stinking, disease-filled collections of hovels and stables. Life for most in the ancient world was difficult and dangerous, devoid of comfort, leisure, pleasure, or hope. Times were terrible before Christ, much more terrible than we moderns can even conceive. Times have always been terrible in this world.

Unfortunately, this one statement by Paul to Timothy has so gripped the evangelical mind that it has obscured many other Scriptures and the wonderful teaching of the Bible—the gospel of Jesus is the power of God unto salvation, a salvation that transforms not only the believer, but his life and consequently his society. Therefore, too many in the church have failed to realize that Jesus changed forever the character of life in this world, to the glory of God.

Granted, this change has come slowly, too slowly, but the cumulative impact of Jesus upon the societies of the world has been phenomenal. Furthermore, His impact is increasing dramatically. Granted, all is not well. Terrible things are still happening everywhere in this world. Nevertheless, there is no question that in nations where the Gospel has gone and been accepted, life today is the best it has ever been in the history of mankind. Never has peace been enjoyed by so many for so long. Never has education been so accessible or extensive. Never has healthcare been so available and so effective. Never have homes been so comfortable and well equipped. Never have food and clothing been so abundant. Never have families enjoyed so much leisure time and had so many toys to play with. Never has travel been so safe and easy and enjoyed by so many. Never has wealth been so abundant and distributed among so many. Never have communication and information been so easy and extensive. Never have women and children been treated with so much honor and care, and never have people lived so long or so well. Never has there been such a worldwide concern for justice and human rights and even animal rights. Never have these concerns impacted political decisions in the highest places as forcefully as they do today. In spite of all the evil activity in this world, these days are not the worst of times. For those privileged to live where the Gospel has had full expression, these are the best times the world has ever experienced.

This book makes no predictions about the future of the world, but when one considers just how much Jesus has improved our culture and comfort, education, science, medicine, and general living standards, we can be very optimistic about the future. As the kingdom continues to increase and the numbers of believers increase in all nations, will not their living conditions vastly improve? Will they not raise grateful voices in praise to God? Will not the Christian message, in spite of evil's intense opposition, continue to change our world for the better, perhaps beyond anything we can imagine, until Jesus comes again? This is a positive, hopeful, totally realistic, and biblically inspired expectation.

Scripture tells us that God has elevated Jesus...

"...far above all rule and authority, power and dominion, and every title that can be given, not only in the present age, but also in the one to come and placed all things under his feet and appointed him to be head over everything for the church, " (Ephesians 1:21–22)

Clearly, God intended the kingdom/church to be the true agent of change in this world. History has demonstrated that truth, but the kingdom's great contribution to our society's improvement is not all in the past. It is the contention of this book that today the church, rather than weakening as many claim, is more alive, active, and effective than it has been since its earliest days. This contention is based, not on anecdotal evidence or wishful thinking, but upon solid scriptural teaching, abundant historical evidence, and up-to-date documented information. The church today, by its energetic efforts, evidences the truth of the ancient prophecy that there shall be no end to the increase of Messiah's kingdom. The Zeal of the Lord Almighty is accomplishing this. (Isaiah 9:7) It is becoming increasingly apparent that Jesus' return will not be to rescue a decimated, defeated church out of the grasp of a powerful, victorious, evil world. Rather, at his return, Jesus will be greeted by vast multitudes of believers, vibrant and victorious. They will glorify Him as the Creator of this marvelous world, their triumphant Kinsman Redeemer King.

"See, darkness covers the earth and thick dark-ness is over the peoples." (Isaiah 60:2)

Two

The World Into Which Jesus Was Born

Life for many in the twenty-first century is incredibly better than and different from life in the world into which Jesus was born. The vast majority of us have no comprehension of how terrible life was at that time. Thus we have very little appreciation of the impact that Jesus has made on the societies of this world.

Imagination fails us in trying to conceive what life was like for the citizens of the ancient world. At the time of Jesus' birth, life for most people in the world was a painful and brief experience. Everyone, including the wealthy, was acquainted with darkness, drudgery, dirt, disease, and death. Violence, cruelty, and ignorance plagued their days and fear haunted their nights.

This chapter examines several aspects of life in the ancient world: family life, city life, educational concerns, and health conditions. The impact of wars, ignorance, and violence upon the societies and culture of the ancient world is also discussed. This look at life in the world into which

Jesus was born will make clear the great difference that Jesus has made and is making in our world.

Villages And Cities

Bethlehem, where Jesus was born, was a very ordinary village. It was no different from thousands of other cities and towns in the ancient world. It was not the serene and beautiful village pictured on our Christmas cards nor the one created in our imagination by the lovely Christmas carol, "O Little Town of Bethlehem." Neither was it a pleasant town like a typical mid-American village, with wide-paved, tree-lined streets, electric lights, and good sanitation. Rather, it was a dirty, hovel-filled town. Its narrow alleys that passed for streets were deep with the dust and dirt of centuries, continually stirred up by the hooves of countless animals. Rubbish of all kinds and excrement from animals and humans alike polluted every foot of the streets.

The houses in such villages and cities were not the spacious homes that most of us live in and enjoy. Heaton and Harrison describe squalid homes of people in ancient times as patched-up shacks, hovels, ill lit, suffocating, insect-infested, one-room apartments inhabited by several persons and domestic animals. "Streets as such were seldom laid out. They were narrow alleys of about seven feet in width and wound up and down without any particular direction in view."[3] Harrison correctly observes something devotional readers of the Bible often miss. "Old Testament writers seem to have taken for granted the ever-present mud and filth of the city streets (Isaiah 5:25; 10:6), which was augmented by broken pottery, fragments of bricks, household garbage, and ashes."[4] Dead asses were simply dragged along streets and thrown outside the gate (Jeremiah 22:19). There were no medical officers of health to worry about flies and germs.[5] Walking in these alley-like streets was not a pleasant experience in the daytime, much less at night. It would have been difficult to avoid the filth under feet and also that being thrown out the doors by careless housewives.

Accustomed as we are to paved streets, clean air, and spacious, well-ventilated houses, we cannot imagine the terrible stench of the streets or how dangerous to one's health were those dirty towns and cities. It is difficult to decide which was worse: the summer heat with its choking stink from the millions of maggots and flies everywhere feasting on decaying waste and dead animals or the winter rains that mixed dirt, ashes and sewage in the streets into awful inches-deep muck. One can understand why the first courtesy rendered to guests was a foot washing and why Jesus was offended by its absence when he visited the home of the wealthy Pharisee. (Luke 7:44)

Roy Porter, Professor of the Social History of Medicine at the Wellcome Institute for the History of Science informs us that even as late as "…the nineteenth century, towns were so unsanitary that their populations never replaced themselves by reproduction."[6] The only reason that towns grew was that life was so unacceptable in the country that people came to the villages hoping for a better life. Unfortunately, they contacted all the diseases prevalent in the villages. Instead of finding a better life, they found death. Porter noted that towns thus gained a reputation as "death traps."[7]

Excavations indicate clearly that once inside one's house, life was no improvement. "Most people lived in terribly overcrowded and impoverished conditions."[8] Large families, including their sheep, goats, and chickens often lived together in the same insect-infested houses. Nathan's parable to King David, about the poor man and his one sheep that "…shared his food, drank from his cup and even slept in his arms." (2 Samuel 12:3) gives us an insight into their living conditions. It wasn't because he was simply a man who loved animals that his animal slept in his arms. It was because he had no other place for his animals.

Usually the house was a one-room, dirt-floored shack with little light and no chimney for either the cooking fire or oil lamp. Tiny slits high in the walls were the only escape for the smoke and the only opportunity for daylight to penetrate the dark hovel.[9] The one room served every purpose of the family. They slept in their clothes on thin mats on the floor, covering themselves with the cloaks used during the day for protection from the weather. Squatting on their haunches or sitting on the floor, they ate without the use of utensils from one pot, cooking on a small, smoky fire in the middle of the room.[10]

Between the insects that usually accompany animals and those that are normally found everywhere, family life in these unscreened, crowded habitations (one hesitates to call them homes) must have been a very uncomfortable and unhealthy experience. In such homes, if the owner had money to purchase furniture or the skill to make it, there would have been little room for it.

With conditions as they were in the villages and cities of the ancient world, how did Jacob raise twelve sons and one daughter without a single child dying? Perhaps it was because Jacob never lived in a village or city, but always in the country. Even so, given the other conditions impacting the family's health, it was a miracle of God that all of Jacob's children survived to adulthood. God worked a similar miracle in the rapid growth of the Israelites in the land of Egypt as reported in the book of Exodus. This growth amazed and frightened the Egyptians who were subject to all the ills of the ancient world. The children of Israel, by God's grace and power, miraculously survived and multiplied greatly in spite of terrible living conditions and oppressive slavery.

Health And Medical Conditions

In the cities and towns of the ancient world, disease and injury were ever-present facts of life, making most persons miserable and their lives short. In fact, if one escaped sickness and injury and early death, he was fortunate indeed. "Archaeology and palaeopathology give us glimpses of forebears who were often malformed, racked with arthritis and lamed by injuries, limbs broken in accidents and mending awry." [11]

As noted above, domestic animals often were housed in the residences of their owners. Infections and diseases were passed from their animals to the residents and their children. Measles, tuberculosis, small pox, influenza, and colds are only some of the diseases passed from animals to humans. In addition, all these animals contributed to the spread of salmonella and to water pollution, which spread polio, cholera, typhoid, diphtheria, and other deadly diseases.[12] Animal-borne diseases, like the plague, destroyed entire families. Yet no one understood why they and their children died in such numbers. It was just a terrible, hurtful fact of life in the world before Christ was born and for too many centuries afterward. It is obvious from reading the Scriptures that no one in the ancient world had any significant knowledge of the cause and cure of disease. There were some astute and observing persons who made some simple connections between causes and effects. For instance, Solomon wrote, "A cheerful heart is good medicine." (Proverbs 17:22) Nevertheless, that observation is a far cry from understanding the invisible bacteria and pollutants that cause all manner of sicknesses and kill without regard to age, health, or wealth. Scripture is full of references to persons afflicted with diseases, but we readers often do not notice them. In addition to the impoverished, crowded living conditions and poor diets, there were the terrible plagues. They are only historical events for us, but for the people of the ancient world, they were devastating disasters—mysterious, terrible, and frequent visitations upon them for no known reason. They are mentioned in the Scriptures[13] but more often in secular histories. For instance, according to the Greek historian Thucydides, one plague killed a quarter-million soldiers and a similar number of civilians after the Peloponnesian War of 431 to 404 BC.[14] These mysterious plagues devastated every aspect of the society of the ancient world. Rawcliffe in Medicine & Society in Later Medieval England, writing about plagues in England, aptly describes, I believe, their impact upon the ancient world as well. "It is impossible for modern readers truly to comprehend the shock and terror generated across Europe by the plague of 1348–49."[15] These plagues and epidemics hit villages and towns like waves, wiping out entire families, destroying the workers, the planters, and harvesters of the crops. They totally disrupted the economy, creating all manners of problems. One local historian of the times reported that as a result of such a demoralizing epidemic, food shortages created spiraling grain prices. If this were not enough, all "…this was followed by famine, then by an unusually violent outbreak of dysentery and a visitation of plague so virulent that all its victims died within twenty-four hours."[16]

Perhaps the account of a survivor of one of these terrible plagues will make clear the dreadful personal pain that was the common lot of men in the world prior to the birth of Jesus and for many centuries afterward, until the impact of his healing ministry changed their world. "None could be found to bury the dead for money or friendship. They died by the hundreds and all were thrown into ditches and covered with earth. And I, Agnolo di Tura, buried my five children with my own hands." [17]

Although it is difficult for us to even imagine such an existence, we need to realize and remember that these people lived in a world with no comprehension of the causes of disease and no ability to accurately diagnose illness. There were no emergency rooms, no hospitals, no dentists, no well-trained physicians, no effective medicines, and no sedatives of any kind. There was no one to summon in the middle of the night when a child was burning with fever and suffering pain from an earache. There was no one to call when for some unknown reason someone's stomach was extremely painful and swelling extraordinarily just like his neighbor's who just died. There was no one, at least no one who had any thing to offer in the way of hope.

In trying to comprehend what it was like to live in a society with none of the medical knowledge, medical professionals, or technology we now have, it is helpful and enlightening to consider how the ancient Hebrews practiced medicine. Although they were ignorant of almost any accurate knowledge, they tried to help the people who were suffering from illnesses and injuries. Excavations have uncovered evidence of surgical operations by the physicians of ancient times. Skulls were bored into, even sawed apart, probably in attempts to relieve the unbearable pain of pressure on the brain. Heaton ponders their situations and understandably writes: "When we consider the crudeness of the surgeon's instruments and the lack of all antiseptics and anesthetics, the terror of undergoing an operation in Old Testament times hardly bears thinking about."[18]

From as far back into antiquity as we can go, we discover that the ancient world was troubled by the same evils that later Christian-era historians recorded in their times. In many respects, it seems almost miraculous that life, beset by such horrendous obstacles as we have been talking about, managed to continue on this planet. "Evidence from Florence in the late 1420's suggests that the average expectation of life may have been twenty-nine and a half years from birth for women and about one year fewer for men."[19] These few years were punctuated with "discomfort caused by gout, hernias, intestinal parasites, rotten teeth and gums, ulcerated limbs and untreated gynaecological problems."[20]

To say nothing of the cruel, brutal actions of men against each other, which will be discussed next, the threat of mysterious illnesses, the chronic conditions just mentioned, the dangers associated with repeated pregnancies and childbirth made life a very short, painful, and uncertain thing. It may help you appreciate just how much these folks suffered during their shortened lives, if you think back to a time in your own experience when you were bothered by a painful illness or dental problem. Remember how quickly you sought out and found effective medical help. Remember how good the relief from the pain felt. Our ancient ancestors had no such recourse and simply had to put up with it and hope to survive.

The writers of Scripture, knowing nothing different from the common experience, mention as a simple matter of fact many such instances when the ancients suffered helplessly under such circumstances. The wealthy patriarch Isaac lived in blindness for perhaps eighty years, almost one-half of his life. The mobs of people who thronged Jesus for cure of their devastating, crippling, and painful ills should make clear to us how terribly hopeless the battles were they waged against disease and illnesses.

Several examples from Scripture indicate how helpless people were in the face of these difficulties and how long they suffered with them. First, in the Gospel of Mark, a woman is described who had "been subject to bleeding for twelve years and suffered a great deal under the care of many doctors and had spent all she had, yet instead of getting better she grew worse." (Mark 5:26) Then there was the man Jesus met at the pool of Bethesda who had been an invalid for thirty-eight years. (John 5:6) Remember also the man who had been blind from birth. (John 9:1) His whole life had been lived in darkness, probably because those who assisted at his entrance into the world simply were not familiar with basic practices of cleanliness. The sudden way King Herod died after his speech to the citizens of Tyre and Sidon at Caesarea is described in Scripture as being struck by God and eaten by worms. (Acts 12:2123) One will not argue with Scripture that God struck Herod for his pride and wickedness, but the death he died was probably the same one that killed King Jehoram (2 Chronicles 21:18–19), common in the ancient world, but not understood by the unenlightened residents of those times.

This brief picture of the health and medical conditions of the people in the world into which Jesus was born is not a pretty one. It is no wonder that nearly everywhere he went Jesus was thronged by masses of people seeking his healing touch. Many came long distances, carrying their ill with them, for there was no other hope in their world.

Violence

Ancient times were bloody times. The record of men who have either not known God or not submitted to his grace is not a pleasant story. The story of mankind is a bloody story and the Bible is faithful in telling it, but as devotional readers of the Bible, we often read its pages without fully appreciating the actual horror of the events described.

The Jewish prophet, Isaiah, complains that in Jerusalem the persons who were supposed to administer justice were, in fact, murderers. No one was safe from their greed. (Isaiah 1) King Manasseh, responsible for the safety of his subjects, shed so much innocent blood that he filled Jerusalem from end to end. (2 Kings 21:16) In addition to offering his own children as sacrifices to pagan gods, he inspired others to join him in his violent activities, murdering innocent men, women, and children. Ripping open pregnant women and spilling their unborn children onto the ground was a common practice of invaders and despots. Although it is not specifically recorded that Manasseh did this, we can reasonably suspect that he was guilty of this terrible practice. This son of one of Judah's most godly kings did more evil than any other king that sat on the throne of Judah, more evil than the Amorites who lived in the land of Canaan prior to the coming of the children of Israel. (2 Kings 21:10) It is difficult, perhaps impossible even, to conceive what life must have been like for the hapless citizens of his kingdom during his long reign.

King David echoes, I think, what most residents of the ancient cities must have felt throughout much of their lives.

"My heart is in anguish within me; the terrors of death assail me. Fear and trembling have beset me; horror has overwhelmed me…Confuse the wicked, O LORD, confound their speech, for I see violence and strife in the city. Day and night they prowl about on its walls; malice and abuse are within it. Destructive forces are at work in the city; threats and lies never leave its streets." (Psalm 55:45, 9–11)

Even the Lord God took note of the terrible life his people were enduring in the cities of the Promised Land. He spoke through Jeremiah. "This city must be punished; it is filled with oppression. As a well pours out its water, so she pours out her wickedness. Violence and destruction resound in her; her sickness and wounds are ever before me." (Jeremiah 6:6–7)

We need to be reminded that a king in ancient times was not a constitutionally elected official. Reading the historical sections of the Bible leaves one with the conviction that most ancient kings were simply the strongest, most violent, and most ruthless persons in the area. When someone more cunning, more opportunistic, more charismatic, more violent, and stronger than the king came along, the king was assassinated. The new thug took the title of king. All the little kingdoms were simply the extensions of the wicked man at the top. When someone like David or Sennacherib or Alexander was strong enough to force his will on other kings, he became somewhat of an emperor. However, with a few notable exceptions, he was no less a murdering monster than before. Saddam Hussein, the former dictator of Iraq, is an example of the type of person who was king or emperor in ancient times. It is no wonder that the inhabitants of the kingdoms lived very uneasy lives.

Other dangers also threatened the residents of the villages and cities in ancient times besides their king and his cronies. These dangers were even more serious than their desperate fellow citizens who robbed and killed without mercy. The most serious threats to citizens of villages and cities were the enemies and raiding parties that often attacked and destroyed walled and unwalled villages alike.

Consider the actions taken by the patriarchs, Levi and Simeon, Israel's sons, and their brothers in avenging the rape of their sister, Dinah. The story is told in Genesis 34. After making a false treaty with the Shechemites, persuading all the men in their city to be circumcised, Levi and Simeon set on the unsuspecting and recovering men and killed every man with their swords. Their brothers came upon the dead bodies and looted the city, carrying off all their wealth and all their women and children, taking as plunder everything in the houses. It is not unreasonable to imagine that the women and children who survived this massacre were treated with a harshness that made them wish they had died with their fathers and husbands.

Observe David while he waited patiently for the Lord to remove Saul from the throne. Although he had several opportunities to do so, David would not put forth his sword against Saul, the Lord's anointed. He gave no one else that same protection. Consider how he provided for himself and the men who had sought him out and sided with him against Saul. While he was temporarily staying in the Philistine territory, he supported himself and his men by raiding nearby cities. Here is how the Bible reports it.

"Now David and his men went up and raided the Geshurites, the Girzites and the Amalekites. ...Whenever David attacked an area, he did not leave a man or woman alive, but took sheep and cattle, donkeys and camels, and clothes. Then he returned to Achish. ...He did not leave a man or woman alive to be brought to Gath, for he thought "They might inform on us and say, 'This is what David did.' "And such was his practice as long as he lived in Philistine territory." (1 Samuel 27:8–9,11)

It is difficult to imagine the bloodshed that took place in these unfortunate cities. David and his men put every man, woman, and child to the sword. Then they went home to their own camp and families as calmly as a man returns from his day at the office.

The conquest of Canaan is another evidence of the awful violence of the ancient world. The book of Joshua records this conquest and tells the story of the destruction of the inhabitants of Canaan. Chapters 10 and 11 summarize the story in its ghastly detail, repeating over and over again the following words and ideas. "They took the city and put it to the sword, together with its king, its villages and everyone in it. They left no survivors. Just as at Eglon they totally destroyed it and everyone in it." (Joshua 10:36ff) City after city, king after king, man after man, woman after woman, child after child, everyone was chopped to death by the sword.

The writer of Israel's history tells another story that reminds us of the violent character of the ancient world. Some of the descendants of Israel's son, Dan, were looking for a place to settle, when they came upon a "...village of peaceful and unsuspecting people. They attacked them with the sword and burned down their city. There was no one to rescue them." (Judges 18:27–28)

This peaceful village in the hill country was no different from any other village in the ancient world. Raids from neighboring cities or bands of violent men made every village and every home a precarious place to be. In the ancient world, particularly where there was no strong central government, life was especially insecure. "There was always the danger of invasion and oppression. The typical Israelite household had to be ready to defend itself at any time."[21]

One can get a picture of how violent these raids on the towns and cities of the ancient world were by reading the Psalms. Consider Psalm 137. The writer, one of the exiles in Babylon, recalls the troubles his people experienced at the destruction of Jerusalem. He concludes his meditations with these words:

"Remember, O Lord, what the Edomites did on the day Jerusalem fell. "Tear it down," they cried, "tear it down to its foundations!" O Daughter of Babylon, doomed to destruction, happy is he who repays you for what you have done to us–he who seizes your infants and dashes them against the rocks." (Psalm 137:7–9)

Obviously, that is exactly what had happened to his people when they were attacked by Nebuchadnezzar's army and carried off to Babylon. Innocent children were torn from their mothers' arms and swung by their heels until their heads were smashed on the rocks, their lifeless bodies tossed aside like so much garbage while ruthless soldiers raped the women and girls or rushed on, looking for more victims. This must have been a very common part of ancient conflicts. Isaiah writes of the Babylonians that in some future conflict, "Their infants will be dashed to pieces before their eyes; their houses will be looted and their wives ravished." (Isaiah 13:16)

Isaiah tells us in Chapter 37 of his prophecy, that

Sennacherib, the king of Assyria, in the fourteenth year of King Hezekiah's reign, attacked all the fortified cities of Judah and captured them. He sent a large army to Hezekiah at Jerusalem with a message asking for surrender to Sennacherib. Hezekiah was terrified and he had good reason to be. The Assyrians were not noted for their kindnesses to the citizens of their conquered cities. The men and women unfortunate enough to survive the attack on their city were treated so terribly that they must certainly have wished they had died when the city was sacked. We might consider being enslaved as about the worst thing that could happen to us, but it was not the worst thing that happened to them. The conquering kings, before actually killing or enslaving some of the leaders, brought them to their thrones "either in cages or in chains, and then tortured, blinded or burnt them alive. One Assyrian king boasted that he had erected a human column of writhing agony."[22]

It is safe to say that there was not a person, man, woman, child, rich man, poor man, king, or peasant in the ancient world who could, at night, lay his head down to sleep on whatever pillow he might have with a reasonable hope that his home or village would not be violently raided during the night and that he and his family would still be alive in the morning.

In the years of Israel's monarchy and even after the return from the exile, life was harsh for people charged with crimes. The patient justice that we are accustomed to was unheard of. Judgment was swift and punishment severe. For minor crimes, it was usually a public beating. For serious crimes, punishment was either crucifixion or stoning with the populace joining in. If the crime were particularly heinous or the criminal particularly popular or famous, his body was removed from under the pile of stones and impaled or hung in the public view for some time.[23]

Life in ancient Rome was no different from that in

Jerusalem. Before the days of the Caesars, there was no order in the city. Anarchy ruled with armed gangs terrorizing the populace while politicians wrestled for leadership. This violence actually led the besieged public to opt for the authoritarian rule of the Caesars. [24]

Life under the Roman Caesars was also precarious. The famous, enforced "Roman Peace" gave some order to society, but those who committed a crime or displeased officials found vengeance and judgment swift and severe. We are very familiar with Matthew's account of King Herod's bloody massacre of all the boy babies in Bethlehem under the age of two years. (Matthew 2:16—18) There is no record that his unjust actions were ever called into question by Rome. Nor were Pilate's when he took out his wrath on certain Galileans, mingling their blood with the blood of their sacrifices. (Luke 13:1) We do not know the circumstances, but the event is very vividly portrayed to our imaginations. Life was cheap in the ancient world. Blood flowed freely. Luke records that another King Herod put the Apostle James to death by the sword. When he saw how this pleased the Jews, he took Apostle Peter, without any fear of condemnation by a higher authority, intending to do the same thing to him. (Acts 12:1–3)

The abuse that the Lord Jesus received before and during his crucifixion was a normal thing in the ancient world. The treatment Jesus received was the fate of thousands of others as well. The Apostle Paul and his associates were severely beaten, several times, with their backs left torn and bleeding. The cruelty shown to human beings in those years is almost impossible for us in the twenty-first century to conceive. One historian exclaims, almost in amazement and disbelief, "How savage the Roman nature was!" [25] She tells of bloody sporting events where the contestants survived by killing their opponents, cheered on by thousands of bloodthirsty fans. This practice was so prevalent that not even Rome's success on the battlefield in securing prisoners could meet the demand for "contestants" in these horrible spectacles.[26]

The above events are just a very few of those recorded in Scripture and secular history. The information presented here tells about life in ancient times in just the tiny area of Palestine and its surrounding countries. Add to this all the other civilizations and wars of the ancient time. Imagine and feel the suffering of those involved all over the world. Perhaps, then, you can begin to get some idea of the brutality and violence that characterized the world and how it impacted those unfortunate enough to have lived in those times. Jesus, preaching his message of love, must have seemed like a deluded dreamer to people accustomed to such violence. However, as we shall see in the next chapter, Jesus was not a dreamer, nor his everlasting love a failure.

Slavery

The great majority of people in the ancient world knew none of the liberties and privileges we now take for granted. The average person in the pre-Christian world was either a slave or almost one. The prophet Samuel, delivering the Lord's message to the people in Israel, warned them that the king they wanted so much would make them slaves. His warning went unheeded. All too soon, it became a reality.

Even before the monarchy, slavery was common and widespread. God gave Moses laws relative to the humane treatment of slaves. These God-given laws were meant for the protection of the privately-owned slaves, the largest class of slaves in Israel.[27] They were the menservants and maid-servants that Samuel referred to in his warning to the people of Israel. When an Israelite found himself in debt and unable to pay, he could be seized and enslaved. An incident related in Scripture clearly tells us about this practice. A widowed woman was in debt and her family threatened by the person to whom she was indebted. On the prophet's instruction, the widowed woman borrowed empty jars from all her neighbors and filled them miraculously from her one remaining jar of oil. She was then able to sell the valuable oil, pay off her deceased husband's debts, and save her children from slavery. (2 Kings 4:1ff It is such an inspiring story that the average devotional reader, thrilled by the picture of God's gracious provision, misses the awful truth of what happened thousands of times over in the ancient world: Children were commonly taken as slaves to pay the debts of their deceased parents.

The monarchies of the ancient world were not the constitutional or symbolic monarchies with which we are familiar in the modern world. They were cruel and often totally enslaving. The monarchies of Israel and Judah, enlightened by the revelation of the law of God, sometimes were less oppressive than those of the surrounding nations. However, their authority and brutality are pictured in the exchange between Jeroboam and Rehoboam at Shechem when the latter came to be crowned king after the death of his father, Solomon. This interchange demonstrates clearly that the people of Israel were not much better off than their neighbors.

Jeroboam and a large portion of the people of the ten northern tribes went to Rehoboam and said to him, "Your father put a heavy yoke on us, but now lighten the harsh labor and the heavy yoke he put on us, and we will serve you." (1 Kings 12:3–4) Rehoboam's answer graphically describes the ruthless power of the kings. "My father made your yoke heavy; I will make it even heavier. My father scourged you with whips; I will scourge you with scorpions." (1 Kings 12:14)

Because of their vast numbers in the ancient world, slaves are often mentioned in the New Testament. The apostles gave instruction both to owners of slaves and to slaves themselves. These instructions expressed God's love for both the owners and the slaves and were intended to create a fair and healthy relationship between them. Understandably, many have said that the apostles should have called for the freeing of slaves. In considering this objection to the biblical treatment of slavery, we must remember the immense number of slaves in the ancient world and also understand God's method for improving life in this world. He improves society from the bottom up by changing the hearts and lives of men and women, not by executive orders from kings or congresses.

How many slaves were there in the ancient world? No one knows for certain, but there were perhaps sixty million slaves in the Roman Empire alone.[28] Mario Pei, in his foreword to *Empire Without End,* writes that "The Roman economy (indeed, Roman society as a whole) was based on the institution of slavery…Slavery was practically universal in the ancient world."[29] Slavery was universal. Slaves were such a normal part of the ancient world's society that little mention is made of their presence and almost no comment is made about their treatment. The latter was true for several reasons. In the first place, slaves were property and completely at the disposal of their owner. What he did to them was entirely up to him. Secondly, there was no more significant effort made to save a slave whose health was in danger than would have been made to save a beast. Hamilton notes that what was true of the Roman Empire regarding slavery was also true of the Greeks. The entire economy and culture were based on slavery. But "in all Greek literature up to the age of Pericles they never come into sight except as individuals here and there."[30] Hamilton characterizes the Roman poet, Horace, as the kind of person that she would want to live forever, but she said that he never was disturbed by the horrible treatment given slaves, never expressed any concern for their lot, or acted as if he ever even considered them human.[31]

We must not think that slaves' lives were pleasant because there were millions of them or because they were an essential part of the society. Of course, some were treated more humanely than others, but as Pei tells us, "The slave of antiquity, like his counterpart in early American history, was legally a chattel, enjoying no civil or human rights." [32]

Hamilton gives us a chilling insight into the true nature of slavery, telling us a story that Horodotus related about the Persians. Everyone was a slave and everything one normally would consider his own belonged to the king in Persia. A noble dined one evening with the king. After the meal, the king brought in a covered basket and gave it to the noble. Lifting the lid, he saw the head and hands of his son. The king asked if he knew the kind of meat he had just feasted on. According to Horodotus, the thoroughly subjugated noble answered with perfect composure, "I do know, indeed, and whatever the king is pleased to do pleases me."[33]

Common law was that "whatever a master does to a slave, undeservedly, in anger, willingly, unwillingly, in forgetfulness, after careful thought, knowingly, unknowingly, is judgment, justice and law."[34] With this understanding of common law and Herodotus' story in mind, it is easy to understand that a massive number of persons in the world, into which Christ was born, were suffering terribly. We get a hint of their sufferings, but only a hint, in the Apostle Peter's instruction to Christian slaves.

"Slaves, submit yourselves to your masters with all respect, not only to those who are good and considerate, but also to those who are harsh. For it is commendable if a man bears up under the pain of unjust suffering because he is conscious of God. But how is it to your credit if you receive a beating for doing wrong and endure it? But if you suffer for doing good and you endure it, this is commendable before God." (1 Peter 2:18–20)

We get a clear picture of the suffering of slaves by reading the story of the children of Israel before they left Egypt for the Promised Land. The story of their sufferings is told in the book of Exodus. "They put slave masters over them to oppress them with forced labor, and they built Pithom and Rameses as store cities for Pharaoh." (Exodus 1:11)

"They made their lives bitter with hard labor in brick and mortar and with all kinds of work in the fields; in all their hard labor the Egyptians used them ruthlessly. The king of Egypt said to the Hebrew midwives, whose names were Shiphrah and Puah, 'When you help the Hebrew women in childbirth and observe them on the delivery stool, if it is a boy, kill him; but if it is a girl, let her live.' " (Exodus 1:14–16)

The sufferings of the Israelite slaves were so severe that God was moved to say to Moses, "I have indeed seen the misery of my people in Egypt. I have heard them crying out because of their slave drivers, and I am concerned about their suffering." (Exodus 3:7)

Gordon observes that the "beatings the Hebrews endured" and recorded in Scripture "add an unfortunately authentic touch to the situation, for this was standard procedure in ancient Egyptian life for encouraging progress in any kind of work." [35] It is no wonder that the Israelite slaves hated their brutal overseers!

The wonders of the ancient world were not built with the help of powerful hydraulic machinery and giant cranes. Neither were fields cleared and leveled by huge earthmoving equipment. Lowly slaves did it all, under the whips of overseers. Their toil, their groans, their sweat, even their deaths built the palaces of kings and the show places that amaze us still today. When we read in the Scripture that Solomon built the temple as well as several palaces and gardens for himself and his wives, we may not realize all that work was done by slaves. Behind those magnificent buildings and the gold that adorned the city were the toiling, the scourging, the suffering, and the death of thousands of Jewish and non-Jewish slaves. This is plainly stated in the Scriptures,[36] but we hardly notice it. "Nelson Glueck, the distinguished American archaeologist, has discovered vast encampments for 'Solomon's slaves' as they came to be called, in and around the industrial center of Ezion-geber."[37] One can only imagine how many of these helpless slaves died under their cruel treatment, but there is not one mention of their suffering or death in the Scriptures. Why not? Obviously, violence and brutality against slaves was such a common thing in the world before Jesus that it never occurred to the writers of Scripture to mention it. The reign of Solomon, glorious in some respects, had a dark side–the virtual enslavement of his entire realm and of all his and his father's captives. It was against this treatment that the ten tribes, to their own ultimate grief, rebelled.

Family Life

Love is the same in every generation and in every place, but cultures are not the same. Economic conditions and governments differ dramatically. All of these factors impact the way love is formed and how it is expressed or crushed. When we read the Scriptures or historical novels, we understand them in the context of our own experiences. Therefore, we make assumptions about love, romance, and family life in pre-modern times that are most often not true. Most of us have little comprehension of what romance, courtship, and family life were like in the pre-modern world, impacted as it was by ignorance, poverty, oppression, violence, war, disease, premature death, and the degradation of its times.

The descendants of Abraham were blessed by the

instructions given to them by God. The Ten Commandments and all of the laws relative to the creation and maintenance of an orderly society, based on the love of God and the Divine knowledge of men, gave them a great advantage in the ancient world. Yet they were not very attentive to the Lord's revelations or obedient to his commands. The further they strayed from God's revealed will, the more they adopted the ignorant and unenlightened customs of their neighbors. Consequently, their personal lives, their family situations, and their societies became as degraded as their neighbors' lives. These facts are evident and often expressed in the Scriptures. For instance:

" Joshua son of Nun, the servant of the Lord, died at the age of a hundred and ten…Then the Israelites did evil in the eyes of the Lord and served the Baals. They forsook the LORD, the God of their fathers, who had brought them out of Egypt. They followed and worshiped various gods of the peoples around them." (Judges 2:8,11–12)

"Judah did evil in the eyes of the LORD. By the sins they committed they stirred up his jealous anger more than their fathers had done. They also set up for themselves high places, sacred stones and Asherah poles on every high hill and under every spreading tree. There were even male shrine prostitutes in the land; the people engaged in all the detestable practices of the nations the LORD had driven out before the Israelites." (1 Kings 14:22–24)

Sexual immorality played a large part in the religion of the Canaanite neighbors of the children of Israel in the Promised Land. The Canaanite religion, like the Mesopotamian religion, had both male and female prostitutes attached to its sanctuaries who received rations from temple storehouses.[38] God had ordered the Israelites to completely destroy all the inhabitants of the land of Canaan when they occupied it and to destroy all their articles of worship. The Lord instructed them to "Break down their altars, smash their sacred stones and cut down their Asherah poles."(Exodus 34:13) He warned them in the following verses:

"Be careful not to make a treaty with those who live in the land; for when they prostitute themselves to their gods and sacrifice to them, they will invite you and you will eat their sacrifices. And when you choose some of their daughters as wives for your sons and those daughters prostitute themselves to their gods, they will lead your sons to do the same." (Exodus 34:15–16)

God did not want them to come in contact with these pagan and immoral religious practices. If they mingled with them and gave their sons and daughters in marriage to them, they would soon become corrupted by their intimate associations.

Henry Snyder Gehman, the former William Henry Green Professor of Old Testament Literature at Princeton Theological Seminary writes in *The New Westminster Dictionary of the Bible* that the worship of the Canaanite God, Baal, "had its origin in the belief that every tract of ground owed its productivity to a supernatural being."[39] In ways completely foreign to us, they believed the longed-for productivity of the land was increased by sexual activity with temple prostitutes. What an ingenious, satanic idea! Such worship increased the value of the temple coffers while giving sinful man a wonderful opportunity to indulge his sexual urges and promote his financial prosperity at the same time. Not surprisingly, some aspects of the pagan religions were very attractive to Israelite men. Their lusts and fears governed their actions much more than any concern for their wives and children.

Just as detestable to God and destructive to family life as the immoral acts of worship was the companion practice of offering children on the altars to the local gods (idols). Scripture refers to this often. One inspired writer of Israel's history, explaining why the Kingdom of Israel was driven into exile, says, "They bowed down to all the starry hosts, and they worshiped Baal. They sacrificed their sons and daughters in the fire." (2 Kings 17:16–17)

What would the act of sacrificing a son or daughter do to a man's spirit? What would it do to his relationship with his wife? How desperate in their minds and hardened in their hearts did these poor, ignorant farmers have to be to participate in these terrible acts? Obviously, these diabolical pagan religions were devastating to the development of family love and solidarity.

Even when there was a serious and determined attempt made by the kings to encourage their subjects to live by the law of God, it seems that the hearts of men found ways to corrupt and injure themselves and their families. The headship of the home, which God intended for the protection and provision of family members, often became the platform for sinful men to rule and even enslave those within their families. It became a matter of common law and practice that the husband had total authority in the home. He could sell his daughters, divorce his wife without providing any support, and even execute disobedient children.[40]

Like Jacob, Esau, David, and others in Scripture, too numerous to mention, men often had several wives. This fact alone worked against harmonious family living and the development of strong ties of love between husband and wife and between brothers and sisters. Scripture often recorded dissension between siblings in such marriages. The only thing that kept the family together was "the absolute authority of the father."[41]

With all this authority and power being assumed by sinful men, it is natural that the plight of women was very precarious. They had no legal rights whatsoever. In Jewish law, a woman was not a person, but a thing. She was subject to the will of her father until marriage, and then to her husband. She could be beaten. She could be divorced without support for the slightest offense, but she could not divorce her husband under any circumstance.[42]

All of these various forces were so detrimental to the true idea of marriage that by the time Christ came "the very institution of marriage was threatened, because Jewish girls were refusing to marry at all because the position of the wife was so uncertain." [43]

When we read the story of the marriage of Joseph and Mary and observe how kindly and respectfully Joseph treated Mary, we assume that he loved her romantically. Yet that is stated nowhere in Scripture and our assumption may be totally false. This does not mean that there were not marriages that knew love in a romantic sense. Jacob loved his wife Rachel with a romantic and passionate love that we moderns can understand, but the bonds of unity and spiritual intimacy enjoyed by loving spouses today could not have existed between Jacob and Rachel with his having three other wives and more than a dozen children.

It is surprising to realize how seldom writers of Scripture used the word "love" with regard to the relationship between husbands and wives. The Apostle Paul instructs husbands to love their wives and wives to love their husbands. This Christian concept was apparently an entirely new idea in the ancient world. There is not one single mention of a home in the New Testament described as loving or happy. Nor is there a single reference to a happy, married relationship. Joseph treated Mary with respect and compassion, but love is never mentioned in the relationship. The Apostle Peter is said to have traveled with his wife on his journeys, but we are given no picture of their relationship. The same is true of the relationship of Pricilla and Aquila. This is not to say that there were no happily married couples in the New Testament, but all indications are that until Paul began preaching family love, there is no reference to any loving marriages among the Jews or early Christians.

In Greek and Roman societies, the situation with the marriage relationship was even worse than in Israel. Desmosthenes' famous quotation aptly describes married life in Greece. "We have courtesans for the sake of pleasure; we have concubines for the sake of daily cohabitation; we have wives for the purpose of having children legitimately, and of having a faithful guardian for all our household affairs."[44]

As in Israel, women were definitely second-class citizens, if that. Prostitution was a way of life. Fidelity in marriage was unheard of. Those women privileged to live in wealthy homes led solitary lives, completely separated from the business and leisure of their husbands. They had no say in the husband's finances other than those expenses related to the affairs of the household. Wives took no part in public life, never ate meals with their husbands, and never accompanied them to social events. Home and family life were near to being extinct.[45] The delightful companionship of a loving fifty-year marriage where children and grandchildren enhance and enrich the relationship, so common in our day, was unknown to those unfortunate, unenlightened persons in pre-Christian times.

Rome, in spite of its position as ruler of the Mediterranean world, was in a chaotic social state, which historians blame for its ultimate fall. The family, which most persons recognize as the basic social unit and foundation of a stable society, was almost nonexistent among the non-slave populace. Persons were married and divorced with such frequency that marriage had no real significance. There are reports of persons being married over a dozen times. One wonders why they even bothered to marry. "The degeneracy of Rome was tragic...The whole atmosphere of the ancient world was adulterous. The marriage bond was on the way to complete breakdown."[46]

With this breakdown in marriage came a breakdown in other social structures that contribute to a stable and orderly society. Bribery, murder, sexual seduction, incest, debauchery, robbery and every other vices flourished so that no business could possibly count on surviving, no person was safe, even in his own house or own bed. Juvenal called Rome a "nightmare city where men must dread poison when the wine sparkles red in the golden cup. Where no woman is decent and no man to be trusted and all wealth dishonestly got."[47]

With chaos in society and the marriage relationship, children must have been the most abused persons in the ancient world. Children, and consequently civilization itself, paid a high price for such terrible societal conditions.

Barclay, in this regard, speaks of the existence of "a callousness and a cruelty" [48] that permeated pre-Christian society. It is easy to see that in marriages that lasted only months, pregnancy and childbirth would be great hindrances to the lifestyles and babies would be a real problem. There were no laws to protect infants. In fact, the laws made it easy for their destruction. No one seemed to care for them. They could be murdered, abandoned, or sold, if there were persons willing to buy them. Most often, they were simply abandoned to those who would take them to rear for sale as slaves or to stock brothels.[49]

In addition to the breakdown of marriage, other factors in the Roman world made life hazardous for children. The father's authority was absolute. Whatever he needed or wanted from the child he could get. If he needed someone to work in his fields, the child had to do it. If he needed money, he could sell the child as a slave. If the child resisted, he could be beaten, chained, or even killed. If the child was not wanted, he could be killed, exposed to the elements, or taken to the center of the city and abandoned.[50]

Beyond Rome, Greece, and Israel, in fact everywhere in the world, childhood has always been the most hazardous time for the human race. This was particularly true before the coming of Christ. It remains true today wherever his healing ministry has not yet effectively reached. Even when there was natural love for family and children, the tremendous difficulties encountered in raising a family in a pre-Christian society made life hazardous for children. Child mortality is still very high in many areas of the world. It was true in Europe as recently as the industrial revolution. Rawcliffe reports that children often did not live to become adults. They died in large numbers from causes associated with their poverty. Many who were not taken by disease were killed by accidents resulting from their being unsupervised for long periods of time.[51]

Education

Next to the presence of evil in the world, ignorance is arguably the greatest curse impacting mankind. Without knowledge, man is a victim—a helpless victim of his own circumstances, of his own passions, of disease and pestilence, of the physically stronger and cruel, of the unscrupulous educated, of circumstances, yes, even of the weather. Without knowledge, the farmer never knew how to improve his crops, how to preserve his meats and other fruits of his labors, or how to relieve his backbreaking work. Without knowledge, the mother or father never knew how to adequately protect the family from the ravages of infection and disease or get relief from the pain of infected teeth or injuries or save the ill from dying. Without knowledge, men did not know how to free themselves from the wicked strong men who enslaved them or how to govern themselves, if they ever did find themselves free. Without knowledge, man has no understanding of whatever God there might be or how to worship him. Without knowledge he has no awareness of anything better or anything hereafter. Without knowledge, man has no hope.

The ignorance of the vast populations in the ancient world, even up to the time of the Reformation, was appalling. Whatever schools there were in the ancient world were attended by only the privileged few. In almost every society, unquestionably, there were some who could read and write, some who could wrestle with great philosophical issues, and some who could calculate and design and work out intricate mathematical problems. Scripture says that Moses was "educated in all the wisdom of the Egyptians". (Acts 7:22) The first five books of the Old Testament bear that out. Obviously, there were others in Israel who could read and write. Many persons wrote the remaining sixty-one books of Scripture in the Hebrew language. Other passages refer to men either writing or reading. For instance, 2 Kings 22:8–10 tells the story of the Hilkiah, the high priest, finding the Book of the Law during the repairs to the temple of the LORD. It was given to Shaphan, the king's secretary, who "read from it in the presence of the king." Further, King Josiah could read. He gathered all the people from the least to the greatest and "read in their hearing all the words of the Book of the Covenant, which had been found in the temple of the LORD." (2 Kings 23:2)

However, as Heaton points out, "Education, in our sense of the word, hardly existed in ancient Israel, but from an early age a boy was taught to share his father's work."[52] "The Jews had a saying, 'He who does not teach his son a useful trade, is bringing him up to be a thief'."[53] There is no record in the Bible of any child, boy or girl, attending a school. Gower claims "There were no schools as such in Old Testament times."[54] That does not mean, however, that there was no formal education available or given. There were opportunities for boys to attend an "...elementary *bet hasefer* or 'house of the book.' "[55] where they learned to read and write for the purpose of understanding the Torah (The Law of God). "Little place was given to the physical training, mathematics, music, art, rhetoric and philosophy."[56] Boys who showed interest and had aptitude for further study could attend a *'bet midrash'* or "house of study."[57] These young men became known as secretaries and/or scribes. In the days of the kingdom they provided many of the services that attorneys do today.[58] After the exile they devoted themselves almost entirely to the study and teaching of the Torah.[59] With rabbis as instructors, the synagogue, which came into being during the exile,[60] was the closest thing to a school that existed. It "…was not only a house of Jewish worship, it was the focus of community activity–school, religious center, meeting hall and courtroom."[61] By the time Jesus was born, Edersheim says, "There can be no reasonable doubt that at that time such schools existed…"[62] When the Bible mentions teaching, it is usually speaking of the parents (Deuteronomy 6:4–9), the king (2 Kings 23:1–3), or of the priests (Nehemiah 8:2–6) teaching the law of God. There is no mention of education of any kind other than occasional references to teaching the Law of God. Schools of the prophets are mentioned in Scripture, but not described. One gets the sense that they were not actual schools, but rather groups of men, similar to the twelve disciples of Jesus, following a noted prophet, such as Elijah. The lack of emphasis upon universal formal education in ancient Israel became obvious to me when I could find no reference to education in historical works, such as Grant's *The History of Ancient Israel.*[63]

Even in the more politically organized civilizations of the ancient world, "Universal education was but a dream of philosophers."[64] In most all nations in the ancient world, only a few had the privilege of any organized education. In Greece, whose culture is commonly considered one of the most enlightened of the ancient world, education was certainly not available to many. "Greek education has been properly characterized as the "well rounding of the well heeled."[65] Obviously, only those who could afford the education received it. "The Greek educational method was centered largely in individual instruction. Most educational experiences involved master and one or several pupils." [66] Although Rome ruled the world around the Mediterranean Sea and large portions of Europe for several hundred years, the impact of the general ignorance of its leaders and the masses of its citizens is indicated by the fact that it did not produce a single major invention or innovation. However, considerable improvements were made in the production and use of things of a mechanical nature, which were already in existence. [67]

For the masses of men, mostly illiterate, unenlightened, and victims of every ill known to man because of their ignorance, the ancient world into which Christ came was a dark and hopeless place. Mazzolan puts it well for the entire world, I think, writing concerning the Roman scholars Sallust, Livy, and Tacitus, "No hope sustained these historians. No celestial city rose as a viable alternative to the horrors of the era in which they lived. No political faith permitted them to forecast a better future." [68]

When we read such records of the conditions in the world prior to the time of Christ's birth and for many centuries afterward, we wonder how the human race endured and even increased. Leonard Hayflick thinks it is amazing that the human species survived hundreds of thousands of years, more than 99 percent of its time on the planet, with a life expectancy of only 18 years." [69] I do not agree with Hayflick's opinion that the human race has been on earth this long. Historical facts do support his judgment that the life span of men in the pre-Christian world was extremely short. As perilous as times were, as deplorable, even diabolical, as customs were, traces of God's image in man, parental love, faithfulness and trustworthiness enabled the unfortunate sons of fallen Adam to survive. Some, like Joseph, were upright and honest (Genesis 39–50), and others were like the Canaanite mother who would not be dissuaded from getting help from Jesus for her tormented daughter. (Matthew 15:21—28) God has also put in the human heart a tremendous will to survive. In our own nation's history the songs of the Negro slaves expressing determination to carry on despite weariness in body and soul would certainly have resonated in the hearts of many men and women throughout man's long, historic struggle for survival.

In these few pages, I have tried to paint an accurate picture of life as it was in the world prior to the coming of Jesus. We are some two thousand years removed from that wondrous night when the angel announced to awestricken shepherds the good news of great joy that was to be to all people and the angelic chorus gave glory to God and sang of peace on earth to men on whom his favor rests. (Luke 2:10,14) Unfortunately, not all people in our world have heard the good news and experienced the peace the angels sang so joyfully about. Tragically, too many in our modern world still live their lives in conditions somewhat similar to the conditions of those who struggled so hopelessly in pre-Christian times.

Clearly, life in the world where the good news of Jesus has gone is unspeakably wonderful when compared to the lives of those discussed in this chapter. In the next chapter, it will be demonstrated conclusively that Jesus is the reason so many of us in these times live so much better than did our ancient ancestors. He is the reason the angels sang of good news for all people and of peace on earth. He is the reason so many of us have it so good today. He is the reason, in fact the only reason, today's life is better for millions than it has ever been in the long history of civilization.

"Arise, shine, for your light has come, and the glory of the Lord rises upon you." (Isaiah 60:1)

THREE

The Impact Of The Kingdom Of God

Historian Jaroslav Pelikan is unequivocal about the impact of Jesus. "Regardless of what anyone may personally think or believe about him, Jesus of Nazareth has been the dominant figure in the history of Western culture for almost twenty centuries."[70] No one has ever ministered so precisely or powerfully to the basic needs of mankind as has Jesus. Pelikan claims, "The life and teachings of Jesus represented an answer or, more often, the answer to the most fundamental questions of human existence and of human destiny."[71]

The newly born church fully expected Jesus to return sooner rather than later. When he did not return as soon as expected, the early Christians began to rethink Jesus' ultimate purpose in his first coming. They began to understand that the prophets saw the entire world as the object of Christ's love. It may have come slowly, but it dawned upon them that Jesus intended to save more than just the few folks who happened to live in the proximity of the Mediterranean Sea. They began to recognize that the kingdom of God would impact and improve the lives of not only Jesus' followers, but the lives of the whole of civilization. Consequently, Tertullian declared, "We also pray for the emperors, for their ministers and for all in authority, for the welfare of the world, for the prevalence of peace, for the delay of the final consummation." [72] The disciples in the early church certainly had no idea how profoundly the kingdom of Christ would change the world for the better. God's answers to those simple prayers would have astounded them. The changes that have come into this world because of the expansion of the kingdom of God demonstrate that Jesus has already transformed society. The "calendar of Europe, which became the calendar for most of the modern world, evolved into a recognition of this view of the significance of the figure of Jesus as the turning point of history."[73]

Pelikan's view agrees with the truth proclaimed in this book and with the facts of history. This chapter shows why some historians have named Jesus as the dominant figure in the history of Western culture. First, we will look at the incredible impact of the truth that Jesus claimed to personify, which he promised would liberate mankind. Next, we will consider the impact of his love on society and culture. Love, the greatest of all virtues according to Scripture, is the essential nature of Jesus. (1 John 4:8) The act of loving God and one's neighbor, the epitome of all the Law and the Prophets, is the motivation and power of the people known as Christians. Love has enabled them to do what Jesus said they would do—overcome the hatred and the power of hell in the world and its devastating effects. (Matthew 16:18)

The Liberating Truth

The previous chapter ended with a discussion of the ignorance that characterized and victimized the ancient and pre-modern world. We now turn our thoughts to the "Liberating Truth." Jesus was not embarrassed to make incredible claims about himself and his words. Speaking to Jewish believers, he promised, "If you hold to my teaching, you are really my disciples. Then you will know the truth, and the truth will set you free." (John 8:31–32)

To a world that lived by lies and intrigue, Jesus announced an eternal principle: The truth will set men free. He was not speaking only of biblical truth or religious truth or truth regarding salvation through faith in Jesus. He was speaking of truth, all truth. Truth liberates. When Jesus said, "I am...the truth...," (John 14:6), he was in fact announcing to the world that he was not only its Savior from sin and death but its Savior from the enslaving power of ignorance and falsehood. He was announcing himself as the great Liberator of all mankind.

History since the birth of Jesus is the story of Jesus liberating mankind from all the ills that it had fallen prey to through sin and ignorance. Not everyone delivered from the chains and agony with which ignorance had enslaved him is necessarily a believer in Jesus as the Savior of sinners. Nevertheless, the blessings that have come through Jesus are gradually touching all the families of the earth, as the ancient prophecy promised. It will be my task in this chapter to demonstrate that the liberties we now enjoy have been delivered to us by the truth that is Jesus, the truth that comes from Jesus.

The world in which we live today differs markedly from the world into which Jesus came. The freedoms and blessings we now enjoy and take for granted, the ancient world knew nothing of and could not even imagine. Those of us privileged to live in the societies that have welcomed Jesus are uniquely blessed. Although there are still illnesses and serious infections to deal with, we are not threatened by the multitude of illnesses and plagues that decimated previous generations. We are not concerned about going hungry or naked or becoming homeless. We do not have to share our homes with farm animals and fowl. We do not suffer greatly from heat or cold or pain. We can be quite confident that the food we eat is pure and nutritional and the water we drink is safe. Neither do we stumble around in darkness after the sun goes down. We do not wonder how our children or parents are doing in the next village or county or country. We can be in almost constant contact with them. Should we need to visit them, we can go to them quickly and in great comfort and relative safety, wherever they may be in the world. We are not concerned that our city or town will be raided by folks in the next city or town or even those from a far country or that we will be killed or enslaved. We are quite confident when we lie down to sleep that when the sun next rises over the horizon, things will be pretty much the same as they were today.

Our life experiences are entirely different from those of the folks into whose world Jesus came so unobtrusively. Many of these common freedoms and blessings, about which we hardly even think, are ours because of the labor and research done in the great universities and medical schools of our world and the discoveries that brilliant and highly educated scientists have made.

Because of technology "we have reaped myriad benefits."[74] We now live long and healthy lives. We work fewer hours with much less strenuous, backbreaking labor. We enjoy much leisure time, whether we are factory workers or homemakers. We keep cool in the summer and warm in the winter with just the touch of a switch or the setting of a computer.

Because many of these great blessings have come to us from universities and medical research facilities, often from discoveries made by unbelieving, sometimes even atheistic persons, we do not even consider that they might all be directly attributable to Jesus. Nor do we realize that they are, in fact, some of the very blessings promised the entire world in that ancient promise to Abraham. It is the truth of these last two statements that I will now demonstrate.

The entire world, prior to the coming of Jesus, was held in the bondage of ignorance, one of the greatest and most deadly evidences of sin's presence in the world. It is not surprising, therefore, that Jesus, the person who claimed to be truth incarnate, was known as "Teacher." Teaching was one of his most continuous activities. Scripture says "When Jesus landed and saw a large crowd, he had compassion on them, because they were like sheep without a shepherd." (Mark 6:34) What did he do when he looked upon this great helpless, shepherd-less multitude? "He began teaching them many things." (Mark 6:34) His final word, the great commission to his tiny church, contained the significant instruction to make disciples of all nations and teach them to obey everything he had commanded them. (Matthew 28:19–20) That the church was very diligent in obeying the Lord's command is well known and understood. What is not generally known is that the great universities of our day are one of the results of faithful obedience to this command to teach. The early Apostles and their descendants throughout the generations were the originators of the educational benefits we enjoy today. "The church can rightfully boast of being in a sense the mother of universities," so claims the volume, *American Catholic Higher Education*. This claim is well documented. "The names of Balogna, Padua, Prague and Paris shine in the earliest history of intellectual endeavors and human progress."[75] The universities that made these cities famous were all begun by the church. In fact, "The church was the only institution in Europe that showed consistent interest in the preservation and cultivation of knowledge." [76] It is a matter of historical record that for the first twelve centuries of the Christian era, "whatever education there was, was due to the church and her clerics."[77] The clergy were the teachers and the monasteries were the schools.

How did this all happen? Founding universities was certainly not in the minds of the twelve disciples before or after Pentecost. We must give the credit for this development to the disciples' obedient response to the leadings of the Holy Spirit as the church grew. Consider how it came to be.

According to Acts, Chapter 1, when Jesus ascended to Heaven, he left a group of men and women disciples numbering about a hundred and twenty. The kingdom of God had a very small beginning, but a strong mandate to go and teach. The disciples, enabled by the Holy Spirit, were fervent in both evangelizing and teaching. In only a few years, there were believers even in Caesar's household and in thousands of other households all over the Roman Empire. The instruction of this multitude of believers was a matter of supreme importance. By "the third century a catechumenal system of instruction was instituted by which converts were prepared for Christian baptism in a three year course."[78] Out of this came the realization that young men needed additional training for the ministry and for the accurate defense of the Gospel. It was not long before schools were established for those purposes.[79]

Here we can see a direct line from the evangelistic and teaching efforts of the early disciples to these early cathedral schools and then on to the universities. Sometimes, referred to as bishops' schools, they were originally begun by bishops for the training of their clergy. By the late eleventh and twelfth centuries, some of these clergy training schools had become the first universities.[80] Robert Clouse, Professor of History at Indiana University, validates the direct line between the church and the origin of the universities. "The cathedral schools culminated in the foundation of universities. The first universities obtained their charters from the pope."[81] With some justification the Middle Ages are often referred to as the Dark Ages. Yet even in the Dark Ages, the light of God's liberating truth was shining and its impact increasing. The church was keeping the light burning and expanding its influence. Kibre recognizes and affirms that the church's development of "organized curricula…cathedral schools and eventually university associations is one of the remarkable achievements of the Middle Ages."[82]

The origins of universities in England can also be traced directly to the church. The universities of Oxford and Cambridge, according to Clouse, were very similar to those on the continent. Even the way their chapels are arranged reflects their religious origins.[83]

Reflecting the desire of the Lord Jesus that his truth be taught to every creature, the men of the late Middle Ages, early Renaissance, and Reformation periods who rose to leadership in the church were greatly involved in public education. One of the earliest of these is Erasmus (1466 to 1536). Ulrich claims that he "became one of the first advocates of a systematic training of teachers."[84] Erasmus profoundly influenced education by stressing the importance of well-trained teachers and better teaching methods. His emphasis was upon helping pupils learn, as opposed to just attending school or sitting through lectures. Furthermore, "He infiltrated classical studies with the spirit of exactness, historical criticism, and international perspectives."[85]

Martin Luther, a contemporary of Erasmus, made enormous contributions to education. Although known primarily as a preacher and aggressive defender of the faith, according to Harold J. Grimm, Luther's "entire career was one of teaching. His mission of spreading the Gospel and reforming the church was essentially one of education." [86]

There were two main reasons for Luther's emphasis upon making education available to everyone. The first was his new understanding of man's relationship with God–every man is personally responsible to God. Therefore he must be able to find out exactly what God requires of him. This need lays the foundation for Luther's second reason for educating the masses. If the Scriptures are the sole authority for the knowledge of what God requires of man, then every man must be able to read and understand them for himself. These two reasons further inspired Luther to encourage the study of languages in the universities so that the Scriptures could be read as they were originally written.[87]

Although Luther's theology was his personal impetus for the furtherance of education, he did not limit his study or encourage others to study only the Bible. His confidence in God as the God of creation and the God of all truth, not just religious truth, led Luther to desire to understand all truth. Consequently, as Grimm points out, "Most unusual for Luther's day was his advocacy of the study of science."[88] Perhaps, more than anyone in his time, Luther realized how the Liberating Truth of Jesus was impacting the world. He saw the dawn of an improving era brought about by an increased understanding of the world around us. He encouraged the search for knowledge, wherever it could be found. He was not afraid that truth would undercut the Christian faith. Since God was the God of creation and Jesus was truth incarnate, truth would only illuminate and bless, not destroy. Truth could only increase our knowledge of God. It is not strange then that he supported efforts to build libraries where information could be readily available to students and people of limited means. "Well known are his tireless efforts in obtaining money for the purchase of books for the library of the University of Wittenberg."[89] Beyond that, relying on his powerful influence as a revered Christian leader, he encouraged the councilmen in cities all across Germany to found and maintain good libraries.

John Calvin, another of the early leaders of the Protestant Reformation, was as concerned with educating the masses as were his peers. Calvin especially recognized the crucial role of an educated ministry in imparting the knowledge of the Christian faith to all believers. For this reason "he pressed for the establishment of a university."[90]

Later John Wesley, the Church of England cleric whose impassioned preaching and teaching in fields and open places ushered in what became known as the Methodist Revival, was himself, "a pioneer of popular education. He conducted educational enterprises continuously for over fifty years."[91]

Once again, the line between Jesus and our modern universities becomes visible. Once again, we see a citizen of the kingdom of God proclaiming the importance of making the Liberating Truth known and available to everyone. Some educational historians maintain that Wesley was "the only leader of importance in eighteenth-century England who had a real and practical interest in educating children of all classes."[92] Wesley was not the only one interested in education, but his lifelong emphasis upon it created the movement for popular education that is still going on today. Because of Wesley, education, even higher education, was no longer considered something only for the rich, but the privilege and right of every person.

Most of the great American universities of today do not consider themselves Christian enterprises. In fact, many would probably reject that idea most enthusiastically. They probably do not see any connection between themselves and the one who proclaimed himself to be the Truth. However, the fact remains, the first universities established in what is now the United States were all established by the church. "At the time of the Revolution, nearly every major Christian sect had a degree-granting institution of its own."[93] The University of Pennsylvania, Harvard University, Yale University, Dartmouth College, as well as Princeton, Brown, Rutgers, Columbia Universities, and the College of William and Mary were all established by citizens of the kingdom of God for the advancement of the knowledge of God. The wonderful liberating blessings that continually come to us through these and other great educational institutions are gifts from Jesus, who said, "You shall know the truth, and the truth shall set you free." For too long we have failed to recognize and appreciate that fact.

Our modern technological world has its basis in truth uncovered by science. Everyone acknowledges that we are all beneficiaries of modern science and the magnificent work of scientists in every field. What is not commonly realized is that the Scientific Age was ushered in by the church. Although there are different judgments among historians as to when to pinpoint the beginning of the Scientific Age, there is ample evidence that it arose out of the church, rather than in opposition to the church as some have claimed. I do not deny that the "official" church sometimes resisted the new understandings and discoveries of its own people. It often excommunicated its own clergy. What critics of the church have failed to recognize is that such instances are examples of the mother rejecting her own offspring. As Alfred North Whitehead and others have claimed, "Christianity is the mother of science."[94] In 1925 at Harvard University, Whitehead gave the Lowell Lectures entitled "Science and the Modern World." In these lectures, Whitehead claimed that Christianity is the mother of science because of the church's insistence on "the intelligible rationality of a personal being."[95] This conviction, according to Whitehead, gave the early scientists confidence "that every detailed occurrence can be correlated with its antecedents in a perfectly definite manner, exemplifying general principles."[96] We readily recognize that this foundational belief underlies all scientific efforts. Without it, the scientist can have no confidence that his experiments will have any reliability or meaning.

For the Christian, science is the search for truth, resident in the intelligent and personal Creator God and established in the universe. Jesus claimed to be Truth Incarnate. Truth is truth. Whatever science discovers to be true can never, therefore, contradict any other truth. No discovery of science can ever contradict who or what Jesus is. No one should ever be afraid of the truth or of the search for truth. Every new discovery in the scientific laboratory or on a planet in space throws some light on the person of God, not as completely as does the Bible, but just as surely. This conviction freed and motivated the first scientists to search out the mysteries contained in the heavens and the earth. This conviction gave rise to the Scientific Revolution and greatly inspires Christians today to involve themselves in scientific endeavors of every kind. Traditionally, the Greeks and the Renaissance have been credited with the radical transformation between the ancient world and the modern world. It makes one wonder; if Greek thought is the truth behind our modern world, why it did not change its own age? It could not and it did not give rise to the modern scientific age. In fact, Greek influence on the theology of the church caused the church to oppose its own children when they were making discoveries that opened the door to our modern world. Their discoveries did not contradict the Bible, although church leaders thought they did. The contradictions were with elements of Aristotelian thought that had wrongly become orthodox Christian thought.[97]

James R. Moore, of the Arts Faculty at the Open University, Milton Keynes, England, has made a significant observation about the correlation between the Protestant Reformation and the birth of science. The leaders of the Reformation, Luther, Calvin, Zwingli, and Knox lifted men's thoughts from a human-centered world to a God-centered one. At the same time, encouraged by these leaders of the Reformation, other believing citizens of the kingdom of God replaced a belief that the universe was centered on the earth with one centered on the sun. "A religious reformation and a scientific revolution went hand in hand."[98] As further evidence of this fact, consider the people who carried the scientific revolution forward. They were all citizens of the Christ's kingdom by personal profession. Moore mentions these notable persons who did everything possible to support astronomer Copernicus, even to the point of subsidizing and publishing his De revolutionibus (1543): Duke Albrecht of Prussia, theologian Andreas Osiander, mathematician Joachim Rhaeticus, Wittenburg professor Erasmus Reinhold, renowned astronomer and Reformed minister Philip van Lansberghe, and Isaac Beeckman, a scientist and devout Calvinist.[99]

Furthermore, inspired by a Moravian educator, in 1645 ten scientists led by Theodore Haak began meetings that only fifteen years later became the Royal Society of London. Seven of these scientists were Puritans. The Puritans demanded "that nature should be studied systematically, rationally and experimentally for the glory of God and the good of mankind."[100]

How reasonable it is to recognize that all the blessings that have come from scientific endeavors for the "good of mankind" came because Christians believed in a rational personal Creator and studied him systematically and rationally, enthusiastically following wherever their discoveries led them! How their discoveries of truth have enriched and liberated mankind!

If these reputable historians are correct, then the conclusion seems unavoidable. Modern science, which ushered us into this truly wonderful age, is the child of the church. Modern science is Jesus' gift to the world. He never used the word science, but boldly said, "I am the truth" (John 14:6) promising that if we would hold to his teaching, we would know the truth, and the truth would set us free. (John 8:31) Jesus was correct. His promise is being realized. The truth has indeed given us wonderful freedoms. We are free from darkness and cold and slavish work because of the truth of electricity. We are free from dependence upon horses for travel because of the truth of mechanical engineering. Because of truth discovered by scientists, we are free from most of the dread diseases of the world, and largely free of the pain formerly associated with dental and surgical procedures. We have the freedom and privilege to travel on the worldwide web and buy and sell around the globe almost instantaneously because of the truth Jesus has made known to us through the efforts of our contemporaries. The truth is continually giving us more and more freedoms.

Because the disciples of Jesus took so seriously his command to go and teach, we enjoy wonderful freedoms that the incredible discoveries in every scientific field have given us. The Congregationalists, the Puritans, the Presbyterians, the Baptists, the Roman Catholics, in fact, every Christian denomination has started colleges and universities, in Europe, in this country, and wherever into the world they have gone with their missions.[101] Wesley, Knox, Calvin, Luther, Erasmus, Newton, Copernicus, and Galileo are only a few in the long line of disciples tracing all the way back to Jesus, who paved the way for the freedoms and pleasures we now enjoy.

The next time you board an airplane for a quick and easy trip to Europe or Asia, turn on your television and watch an event live from some remote spot on the globe or even outer space, switch on your computer and check your bank account or stock portfolio, chat on the Internet or over your cell phone with someone in Europe or Asia, or the next time you swallow a pill that will help your body throw off what used to be a fatal disease, realize and remember that you are enjoying these liberties and these blessings because of Jesus who said, "I am...the Truth..." (John 14:6) Jesus is the one of whom God spoke to Abraham, promising him a son through whom all peoples on earth would be blessed.

(Genesis 12:13) We Christians need to recognize that our freedoms and gifts are some of the blessings promised to all the world through Abraham's heir, Jesus. Too long we have looked to Abraham's seed only for "spiritual" blessings. In so doing, we have given credit to others rather than to Jesus for our modern freedoms and all the "physical" blessings we so enjoy.

The Healing Love

When thinking of the pre-Christian world, it is difficult to decide which was the greater curse: ignorance or brutality. Remembering the discussion on family life in ancient times and the discussion on slavery, we realize that brutality was more than just a way of life. It seemed to be inherent in mankind. Much evidence in the modern world suggests that mankind has not changed all that much, but society certainly has. How can the change in society be explained, when the men who make up that society are still capable of almost unbelievable insensitivity to and violence against each other?

There is, to this student, only one answer: the love of God that came into the world in the person of Jesus and became resident in the hearts of believers the world over. This love, personified in Jesus, motivates every effort to relieve suffering and restrict brutality and violence. This same love has sensitized the conscience of nearly everyone, even non-believers in Jesus, to the pain and needs of others and to the dehumanizing influence of violence and ignorance. Jesus' impact upon society has been so pervasive and effective that society has moved to the point of even having societies for the prevention of cruelty toward animals.

Previously we noted how many recognized historians consider the church to be the mother of the modern university and the mother of science. Now we will demonstrate that the positive change in the world's attitude toward men, women, children, and yes, even toward animals, can also be traced back to Jesus. The love of God, resident in Jesus, manifesting itself through his church, has joined hands with the liberating truth also resident in Jesus to gradually lift a large portion of civilization out of its desperate and almost unbearable plight. The kingdom of God is transforming the world.

The Earliest Expressions Of This Love

Two convictions gripped the hearts and minds of the earliest Christians. One was the strong anticipation and expectation of the imminent return of Christ. The other was concern for the ill and infirm among them. When one anticipates that Jesus will perhaps return today, there is little motivation to do more than make the suffering person comfortable. Certainly, with that mentality the motivation to understand the causes of illnesses and look for cures would not be strong. However, as the church began to realize the worldwide intentions of God, it began to take a more dramatic interest in the needs of the sea of suffering people around it. As is reported in *MEDICINE, An Illustrated History,* "Concern for the problems of everyday life returned as the end of the world proved less than imminent. Prime among these were considerations of health and disease."[102]

Although compassion for the poor and ailing was in scarce supply and the knowledge of the causes of disease and medicines very limited, there were hospitals prior to the advent of Jesus. In most instances, the motivation for these medical centers does not appear to have been love. "Roman physicians' skills were stimulated by the medical needs of the Roman army."[103] In India, there were hospitals for the poor, but undoubtedly, the most common reason for the creation of a hospital was the needs of the rich and royal, as suggested by the account of Megasthenes, ambassador from the eastern Greek Seleucid king.[104] When Christians ministered to the sick, they ministered to everyone, rich and poor, military and nonmilitary, child and adult, free and slave, old and young.

Our world and the ancient world have this in common. The needs of poor widows, orphans, and the sick are greater than individuals, by themselves, can satisfy. Consequently, the church, as seen in the sixth chapter of the book of the Acts of the apostles, began to assume this responsibility. As the kingdom increased in numbers, it increased in ministry as well. Everyone shared in the ministry of providing for those in need. Wealthy converts saw their wealth as a trust from God and worked faithfully to assist where they could. Roy Porter, Professor of the Social History of Medicine at the Wellcome Institute for the History of Science, tells of one such person—a woman named Fabiola. Although accustomed to the refinements that accompany wealth, she went out into the city's most degraded areas and gathered up the sick and dying. No matter how terrible and disgusting their conditions, she brought them to a home that she had established and personally cared for them as if they were her own family. Her teacher, St. Jerome, said, "I have often seen her washing wounds which others, even men, could hardly bear to look at, lost eyes, mangled feet, ailing flesh filled up with hungry worms."[105]

According to Porter, "Greek and Roman paganism had acknowledged no such duties."[106] Lyons observes that Greeks and Romans cared little for persons whose illnesses were beyond their ability to cure. "If the ill patient could not be cured or at least improved, he was virtually abandoned by the physician as well as his neighbors." [107] "The hopelessly ill and deformed were little cared for. The same disdain extended to unwanted newborns and led to their disposal."[108] William Barclay agrees with this assessment. Pre-Christian civilization was merciless. Sickly or deformed children were ruthlessly put to death. It was common practice in the world before Jesus and for too long after his coming.[109]

Aside from the military and wealthy and easily cured, the vast majority of sick were neglected or destroyed by the ancient un-Christian world. The advent of Jesus began to change all this. The love of God that indwelt the disciples of Jesus caused them to see in the parable of the Good Samaritan the "model of the benevolent person performing good works out of compassion for his fellow man."[110] We recognize that this concept underlies all Christians in whatever charitable endeavor they are involved. Wherever Jesus' disciples went, the healing ministry of Jesus also went. Actually, the self-sacrificing ministry of these early disciples demanded more of themselves than the healing miracles Jesus performed demanded of him. However, their faithful sacrificial labors on behalf of the poor, hungry, injured, and ill greatly glorified the Lord Jesus who dwelt in them.

Do you want evidence that it was love of Christ in the church that has given us the great and wonderful hospitals we appreciate so much today? Then note what happened after Constantine officially recognized Christianity. Public facilities for the administration of love—hospitals, homes for foundlings, orphans and the elderly and the poor—were created all over the Roman Empire. St Basil erected outside the walls of Caesarea "almost a new city" for the sick, poor and leprous.[111] Porter rightly says, "The Christian hospices were the first ever to be devoted to long-term support of the diseased, poor, and downtrodden."[112] No other society or culture anywhere else in the pre-Christian world had done what the church did in caring for the distressed, the poor, the sick, the injured, and the dying. These early Christians laid the foundation for what later became the rule of life for such Christian orders as the Benedictines. For them, "The care of the sick is to be placed above every other duty, as if indeed Christ were being directly served by waiting on them."[113]

Not surprisingly, "...monasteries became key medical centers."[114] We may be surprised to realize that our great hospitals and medical research centers are but the modern expression of those ancient relatively ineffective centers for the care of souls and bodies. We need to recognize that these efficient wonderful medical centers today are more than the product of scientific discovery. They are first and foremost, the results of the love that came into our world through Jesus.

Furthermore, it can be well argued that had there not been the passionate desire to relieve suffering that God's love generated, there would not have been motivation to discover the causes and cures of diseases nor the desire to minister to everyone in need. A definite indication of this truth is the fact that when the church first began to transfer its hospitals over to municipal authority and the care of the sick became a job, rather than an expression of love, "...hospitals tended to become filthy, germ infested buildings where people often died of infection rather than the illness which brought them there."[115] It was the love of God that created hospitals. It was the love of God that kept them clean. It was the love of God that made them healing institutions. These facts are indisputable.

Later Expressions Of This Love

As genuine, sacrificial, and ambitious as were the efforts at relieving the suffering of their day, the early Christians did not make much of a dent in the world's overwhelming sea of suffering. For well over a thousand years after the birth of Christ life expectancy was very short and life's experience for most was one of great physical discomfort from a variety of unexplained and painful debilitating illnesses. The need was overwhelming and continuous. Progress was slow and faltering, but the disciples of Jesus persisted, in spite of ignorance and wars and oppression and even persecution. There were many side roads leading down dead ends and many deviations from the truth that embarrass us Christians. For instance, St. Benedict of Nursia encouraged the care of the sick in founding his order as the Monastery of Cassino. As noted previously, the Benedictine rule states that "the care of the sick is to be placed above and before every other duty, as if indeed Christ were being directly served by waiting on them."[116] Unbelievably, Benedict forbade the study of medicine, because he believed "the cure of disease was possible only through prayer and divine intervention."[117] The devout and blessed St. Bernard of Clairvaux (1090–1153) "asserted that to consult physicians and take medicines befits not religion and is contrary to purity."[118]

Although ignorance still plagued the disciples of Jesus, the love of God resident in his people kept them doing what they could for the sick and suffering. For several centuries, "…the hospital sphere long remained largely the church's responsibility." [119] Porter reports that there were very large and complex Christian hospitals in Jerusalem, Constantinople, Edessa, and Antioch. In Constantinople, there was also a teaching facility for medical personnel as well as a home for the elderly. Outside of the city walls, the Christians maintained a home for lepers.[120] By medieval times, there were hospitals and medical foundations everywhere in Europe and England. In spite of the foolish prohibitions against physicians and the study of medicine by Benedict and Bernard and others, "Medieval hospitals were religious foundations through and through. Within hospital walls, the Christian ethos was all-pervasive." [121]

Those opposed to the Christian message delight in pointing to some of the embarrassing stands of the early Christians to espouse "…the view that the church arrested medical progress."[122] However, says Porter, "Such judgments miss the mark. Medieval hospitals have been criticized for their religious ethos, but without the Christian virtue of charity would such hospitals have existed at all?" [123] The answer is, "No, they would not have existed." The world had hundreds of years before the coming of Jesus to establish hospitals and to endeavor to relieve the suffering so common to its existence. However, except in few brief instances where hospitals were created for the wealthy and military, they did not. Instead of mercy and ministry, unabated unconcern, brutality, and violence characterized the pre-Christian world.

Christians acknowledge that ignorance on the part of the disciples of the Lord slowed the advance of medical knowledge. As Jesus disciples continued to hold to his teachings on love and continued to express that love in whatever way they could, his promise that they should know the truth and be set free by that truth (John 8:31) began to come to pass. It was exactly as Jesus promised. The Christian monasteries that began to care for the sick began to educate the unlearned. The Christian monasteries that mothered the universities also created the hospitals. It is easy to see how it was in God's wisdom and grace that these two powerful Christian social passions would complement each other. The great age of hospital building from around 1200 A.D. coincided with the flourishing of universities in Italy, Spain, France, and England.[124]

While the church was multiplying hospitals and leper colonies, it remained largely ignorant of the cause and cure of disease. The compassion that created hospitals drove Christians to try to understand the causes and cures of the diseases with which they had to deal daily. It is only natural that as universities increased, both in number and size, there was increased desire to expand and teach medical knowledge. Thus it is not surprising that shortly after the cathedral masters received legal recognition for their corporate status as universities in the early thirteenth century, they began the study of medicine.[125] Although the universities were under the control of the church, the teachers in the medical schools were no longer bishops, abbots, and priests.[126]

The great medical schools and teaching hospitals of our day are a far cry from the church's first schools for the study of medicine. Yet they are direct descendants of those early and limited educational institutions. Through them, the blessings promised to Abraham's descendants and the freedoms promised by Jesus are now being realized to an extent that amazes even us moderns.

The church did not limit itself to ministering to those afflicted with the more ordinary ills. It also reached out to the mentally ill and the lepers, those who were often neglected, shunned, or imprisoned. The Quakers were in the forefront of this ministry. Among these was the English Quaker William Tuke (1732–1822), who established the York Retreat for the humane care of the mentally ill. "This pioneer institution set a pattern which was soon adopted in many parts of Europe."[127]

Many other Christian persons heavily involved themselves ministering to the mentally ill as well. Dorothea Lynde Dix (1802–1887), in England and the United States, mounted a personal campaign that eventually achieved the transfer of the mentally ill from brutality and negligence in penal institutions to psychiatric hospitals with more appropriate nursing facilities. Eliabeth Gurned Fry (1780–1845), an English Quaker, organized the Society of Protestant Sisters of Charity in 1840, which attempted to send nurses into the homes of the sick, whether rich or poor. Theodor Fliedner (1800–1864), a Lutheran minister in Germany and his wife, Frederika, were influenced by Fry's work. In 1835, they established a modest hospital in Kaiserwerth, staffed without pay by the deaconesses of his church, in which the character, health, and education of nurses achieved a high standard.[128]

From ancient times to the Middle Ages, lepers were universally excluded from participating in the life of the communities in which they had previously lived. Bible stories tell of the devastated lives of the lepers of the ancient world. This treatment of incurable lepers continued throughout the Middle Ages. Usually "all individuals called lepers were subjected to total ostracism from society."[129] It took the church a long time to effectively minister to lepers and change this inhumane practice. Here again, as in every other effort to relieve the suffering, the love of Jesus, through his disciples, evidenced itself. "The Order of Lazarus was so sympathetic to the care of lepers that Lazarhouse quickly connoted leprosarium and thousands were soon built throughout Europe."[130]

The list of Christians who have greatly blessed our world is endless. Ministering to the dying on the streets of ancient Rome, searching for the cures of diseases, fighting against the misuse of alcohol, tobacco, and drugs, improving conditions of prisoners and the insane, ministering to slaves, working for racial justice and equality–in all theses endeavors Christians have been diligent and persistent laborers. The modern facilities for the mentally ill and the leprous the world over, the great prison complexes where men, women, and children are treated humanely with kindness, and the great charitable institutions in the world are here primarily because the church cared.

Certainly, not everyone today who advocates for the humane treatment of the mentally ill and prisoners is a believing Christian. However, the love of Jesus, expressed in the lives of his followers, has sensitized the consciences and minds of modern men to the needs of their neighbors and to the importance of immediate and meaningful relief to victims of disease, poverty, crime, war, natural disasters, and the importance of humane treatment of offenders. Clearly, the areas of the world where the kingdom of Jesus has significantly impacted society are vastly better and kinder places to live than the world into which He came and the places in today's world where He is not yet welcome.

In the next chapter, we will look at the present day ministry of Jesus. His Spirit-anointed church is making incredibly successful efforts to reach all the peoples of the world with Jesus' transforming truth and love. It is an exciting and encouraging picture.

"God placed all things under his feet and appointed him to be head over everything for the church, which is his body, the fullness of him who fills everything in every way." (Ephesians 1:27)

FOUR

The Expansion Of The Kingdom Of God (The Twenty-First-Century Church)

In the previous chapters, we examined the impact that the kingdom of Jesus has had upon the societies of our world. We have seen that Jesus, through his kingdom/church, has been transforming life on earth—lifting humanity from ignorance, violence, degradation, disease, grinding poverty, and premature death to a plane where life for most is comfortable, enjoyable, and for many is almost luxurious.

We move now to look at Jesus' ministry today. What is the condition of his kingdom/church now? Has it lost its sense of mission and its zeal to evangelize? Has it become callous to the physical and social needs of the world's peoples? Is it still making a powerfully positive impact, or has it been overcome and inundated by its own successes and affluence, as many claim,[131] and fallen into a state of passivity and irrelevance?

My conviction is that, in harmony with the great and consistent prophecies of Scripture, the kingdom of God is making more of an impact than ever upon the world. It is advancing against the outposts of evil on a worldwide front with considerable success. The Apostle Paul's words to the Christians in Colosse are as true today as they were then. "All over the world this Gospel is bearing fruit and growing, just as it has been doing among you since the day you heard it and understood God's grace in all its truth." (Colossians 1:6) Using the analogy of a military expeditionary force, Christ's kingdom is advancing against the enemy on a global front on the ground and through the air with every means and weapon that God provides—now to substantiate these claims.

I will not attempt to gauge the strength and influence of the church by counting its members or its recent converts. The number of members of the churches seems to be almost irrelevant, considering the differing standards for membership. What does seem relevant is how the church confronts and overcomes the brutality and spiritual darkness that still drag down the world's peoples. This chapter will focus on that vital subject.

John Bright wrote in 1950 that "The Kingdom of God is a power already released in the world." He added a strong affirmation, "Nothing can stop it." [132] I hope, after considering the information presented here, you will agree. The kingdom today is far from being passive or stymied. It is making a positive difference in this world. Indeed, all the powers of hell combined have not been able to stop its progress. In fact, the kingdom is picking up speed and gaining momentum.

Clouse, Peirard, and Yamauchi note that during the nearly 400 years since the first settlers arrived in Massachusetts, there were about 58 mission organizations formed worldwide. [133] In the 50 years since mid-century, according to *The Encyclopedia of Associations,* 88 new mission organizations have been organized to spread the Gospel.[134] Many of these new missions are now worldwide effective servants of Christ. We will note just a few of them.

In spite of the tremendous advance of the kingdom of God, instead of the excitement that characterized the utopia-minded, late nineteenth-century church, many in the evangelical church are deeply discouraged. Even a man whom God has used to reach thousands of persons for Jesus makes the astoundingly discouraging assertion, "Not since the barbarian hordes overran Europe has the influence of Christianity been weaker."[135] It amazes me that there is so little recognition of how the Gospel of Jesus has lifted people out of their degraded existence and changed their living conditions for the better. Just as surprising is the failure of Christians to see what the church is doing today. I believe that today the kingdom/church is stronger and more effective than it has ever been in all of history. This conviction is based upon concrete evidence. The church has risen out of the ashes of disillusionment following World War I to evangelize and confront evil on a worldwide scale. Note some facts that confirm this judgment.

The church, begun in Jerusalem on the day of Pentecost, now ministers in almost every hamlet and village in the Western World and in much of the East. Through its extensive missions program, the above is also true in many Third-World countries. It was my privilege several years ago to venture into the mountains of Honduras to a tiny village. The village had no school, store, or place of business, but it had a church. Furthermore, the church is active and effective even in countries of the world where political or religious barriers forbid its existence. The gates of political regulation and religious hostility have not been able to shut it out or shut it down. Indications are that the church may even be more vital in these nations than in the nations where it is permitted and encouraged.

The Bible says that the "Zeal of the Lord Almighty"

will advance the kingdom of the Messiah. (Isaiah 9:7) The zeal of the Lord Almighty that Scripture speaks of is evident in the mission organizations that he has brought out of the church in the last fifty or so years. As we look at these organizations, note that each has a very specific ministry to aggressively engage the world or to advance the kingdom. Let us think of God as the Commander in Chief of heaven's armies, directing a tremendous global war against the enemy of all mankind. He has brought into existence each of the following armies and is giving each one incredible success in this world campaign against evil. Please note and praise God for the following new ministries that have arisen out of the church in these exciting days.

Campus Crusade For Christ, International

Established in 1951 by Bill and Vonette Bright as a ministry to college and university students, Campus Crusade for Christ, International (CCCI) has broadened out to minister in many areas of human society. Its stated goal is "to help give every man, woman, and child in the entire world an opportunity to find new life in Jesus."[136] It is actively and successfully pursuing its goal. For instance, Stephen B. Douglass, the newly elected President of CCCI, in his first message to its constituency, reported that the Jesus film, one of CCCI's dramatic efforts to evangelize, has now been translated into well over 700 languages. This film has been shown in every country of the world, accounting for almost five billion exposures to the Gospel.[137] Since that report was written, the total number of languages into which the Jesus film has been translated is now over 800 and growing steadily. The Jesus film is continually being shown all over the world, in jungle villages, remote mountain towns, capital cities, in rebel camps, even in territories where preaching the Gospel of Christ is forbidden. Hundreds of volunteers often risk their lives to carry this wonderful evangelistic tool to others.

In addition, consider some of the other ministries of CCCI. As you look over this list, notice how persons in every walk of life are being given the opportunity to hear the good news of Jesus.

- Arrowhead Productions International, producing radio programs, videos, and interactive multimedia presentations.

- Athletes in Action, using the platform of athletics to proclaim Christ.

- Campus Ministry to college and university students.

- Christian Embassy, D.C., reaching government, military and diplomatic leaders.

- Christian Leadership Ministries, to reach and equip professors to change the world for Christ.

- ChurchLIFE, teaching lay people the Spirit-filled life and training them in evangelism.

- Disciplemakers International, providing resource materials for discipleship.

- Executive Ministries, reaching the executive community for Jesus.

- FamilyLife providing practical, biblical tools to strengthen and build family relationships.

- Global Resources, an International Community Strategy, sending people to the world on short-term mission assignments.

- Women Today International, providing spiritual and intellectual resources and opportunities for women to help them be effective ambassadors for Christ in every workplace and neighborhood.

• Military Ministry bringing hope and resources to the military community worldwide.

Considering the purpose of this chapter, it is appropriate to comment on one of the ministries of CCCI mentioned above, FamilyLife Ministries.[138] FamilyLife Ministries is truly a new work of the Holy Spirit. It does not appear that its originators ever saw its present form or expected its explosive growth. "In 1976, Campus Crusade began Family Ministry to provide pre-marriage seminars for its staff members." Observing the impact of these seminars for unmarried staff members, married couples and pastors wanted similar seminars for married couples. Consequently, Family Ministry, now called FamilyLife, opened the *FamilyLife Marriage Conference* to the public in 1978.

FamilyLife is now global, with conferences held in numerous countries around the world. At the heart of Family-Life are 10,000 lay volunteer couples working with the staff of FamilyLife to sponsor the citywide conferences and lead HomeBuilders Couples Series studies. In 2002, over 100 FamilyLife Marriage Conferences were held in major cities in America. To date, more than one million people have attended the marriage conferences; many more have used the FamilyLife marriage strengthening-materials and attended small group marriage-strengthening meetings. Every day, thousands tune in to the radio program, *FamilyLife Today,* which is heard on major Christian stations around the country.

Bright believed that reaching the family is the best way to reach the world for Christ. Certainly this worldwide ministry of the twenty-first-century church of Jesus is unique in the history of the world. It is one of the new wine skins that the Holy Spirit is using to carry the Gospel and its healing truths to a very ripe harvest field, the endangered homes of this generation.

The ministries listed above are only a few of the

many efforts that CCCI is using to meet its goal of giving every person on earth an opportunity to believe in Jesus. There are approximately 40 other ministries sponsored by CCCI involving 25,000 full-time and over 500,000 trained volunteer staff. CCCI investment in ministry from 1999 to 2001 was over 1.25 billion dollars, most of which came in the form of small donations from Christians all over the world.[139]

Bill Bright correctly referred to these days as "the greatest spiritual harvest of all time."[140] If this were the only army the Lord is using, we could still be thrilled at what Jesus is doing in our day. We could look to the future with much faith and excitement, praising God for so blessing his church. However, Campus Crusade for Christ is only one of the Lord's great armies. Consider also World Vision.

World Vision

World Vision is another indication of the church's present-day vitality. The Lord raised up World Vision to minister to the persons most ravaged by the evils of this world. The breadth of its ministry to devastated people, regardless of their race or religious heritage, is as broad as the need itself. Whether the need be food for the starving or medicine for the ill, new wells for water deprived villages, money to enable a poor person, man or woman, to begin a business, homes, water, and food for victims of natural disasters, World Vision is there.

In 1950 Bob Pierce, a missionary to the Orient, needed to raise funds for orphans in Korea and for missionary efforts in Asia. He began an organization that in just a few years became known the world over as World Vision.[141] As inspired as Bob Pierce was and as confident as he was in God, I cannot believe that he had any idea what God would do with that little beginning. Like the Kingdom of God itself,

World Vision is a healing mustard plant expanding into all the earth, wherever there is a need. Through his compassionate and vital church, Jesus has dramatically increased World Vision's ministry and scope to the point that in 2002 alone it assisted 85 million people in 96 countries. Included in that number are 1.5 million children sponsored through World Vision's global partnership. World Vision's 2002 Annual Report also indicates that in that year over 1.3 billion dollars in cash and goods were donated to World Vision for distribution to the needy people of the world. That which began as a small ministry to a devastated peninsula has become one of the most respected and largest relief agencies in the world. It could not have happened without the continuous sacrificial giving and faithful prayer support of millions of Christians over these past fifty years.

When one reads the Gospels, he sees Jesus walking through the villages and fields of the land of Palestine reaching out and ministering to the suffering persons that flocked to him. When one reads the quarterly magazine *World Vision Today* and sees the pictures of volunteers digging wells, inoculating babies, handing out rice and milk, building houses, giving warm clothing to poverty-stricken mountain children, holding starving children and gently feeding them, ministering to HIV/AIDS victims, working with local and national governments to prevent the spread of HIV/AIDS, rescuing children sold into prostitution, teaching farmers better methods, establishing community seed banks, providing care for orphans, loaning money to individuals to enable them to begin their own businesses, he sees Jesus again incarnate in young men and women, doing what he did in his days on earth. However, in these World Vision volunteers, he is not in the land of Palestine alone. He is everywhere in this world where there is human need. A graphic illustration of World Vision's ministry is its response in December of 2004 to the terrible earthquake and tsunamis that devastated vast areas of Southeast Asia. When the tsunamis hit, there were already nearly 4000 World Vision staff in the area who responded within hours of the disaster. Almost immediately, they sent two cargo ships containing relief supplies of all kinds to the northern province of Indonesia. In India, they provided immediate relief for more than 3000 families and 35,000 more in surrounding areas. Within a month, they had provided nearly 400,000 people with lifesaving aid, such as Family Survival Kits, which included food, water, medicine, sleeping mats, and clothing. In addition, they established children's centers to care for and protect the children who were orphaned, homeless, and traumatized.

Where do these thousands of volunteers come from? They are "Kingdom Kids," the children of the church. They are sent out and supported in prayer by the church. Where does the money come from to support them and provide the material and medical goods they distribute? It is the church's money that enables World Vision to bring healing and hope and relief to so many suffering souls. World Vision is the twenty-first-century church in action, a specially designed division of the Lord's army on the front lines of the conflict with evil, ministering to those most damaged, ministering to those Jesus loves, ministering to those for whom Jesus died.

Prison Fellowship International

Prison Fellowship International (PFI) is another specific ministry that the Lord has created and is using effectively to reach some of the most destitute, lonely persons in the world. Prison Fellowship was begun in 1976 by Charles Colson, chief counsel for former President Richard M. Nixon.[142] After serving time in prison for a Watergate-related crime, Colson started Prison Fellowship to bring Christians together to share their faith and the love of God with prisoners, ex-prisoners, and their families.

Since its humble beginnings, Prison Fellowship has become a widely known, effective avenue for Christians to express their love for God and man. In only three years, Prison Fellowship expanded to several countries, including Australia, New Zealand, and Canada. Thus in 1979 Prison Fellowship International was formed to develop and serve the national Prison Fellowship organizations. Twenty-five years later, there are national Prison Fellowship organizations in 98 countries of the world. In 2002, Prison Fellowship ministered in 7112 prisons worldwide to approximately 600,000 prisoners. Ronald W. Nikkel, President and Chief Executive Officer of Prison Fellowship International, states that there are 800 board members and an army of over 100,000 Christian volunteers carrying out the mission. This army of volunteers transcends every difference and division between men and women of denomination, race, culture, and social/economic status and unites them in this ministry. Michael Timmis, Chairman of the Board of Directors, considers the raising of this army by the Holy Spirit one of the great miracles of all time. PFI received over 1 million dollars in 2002 in gifts from the church. In addition, the 98 national Prison Fellowship organizations receive financial support locally for their ministries. The amount of money invested in prison ministry by the Church since the official beginning of Prison Fellowship totals many millions of dollars.

As a Prison Fellowship volunteer and seminar instructor, I can testify from personal experience that the Holy Spirit is using this ministry in a wonderful way. I estimate that about 10 percent of the approximately 5000 men in the prison I serve most often have responded positively to the message of Jesus through the ministry of Prison Fellowship, in cooperation with local churches.

Prison Fellowship's ministry is much broader than

believers going into prisons to conduct services and seminars. These efforts are an important and wonderful part of the ministry, but not by any means the largest part. The web page of Prison Fellowship International describes other important aspects of its work.

PFI provides general support services including organizational and program consultation, communications, leadership training, program development, criminal justice and restorative justice research, and international representation. Angel Tree, a special outreach to the children of prisoners at Christmas, attracts the enthusiastic support of church families, touching the hearts of church children and sensitizing them to the needs of others beyond their local relationships. In addition to the Christmas project, Angel Tree provides camps, retreats, and a variety of year-round events and support services designed to keep the children of prisoners from becoming involved in a life of crime.

In Brazil, Prison Fellowship has a faith-based prison regimen developed over a process of 30 years of experience. Prisoners volunteer to participate in a graduated program designed to help them experience and participate in responsible giving, loving relationships.

When a prisoner is released from prison, typically the state provides him with a small sum of money, perhaps $50.00, and he is then on his own. With possibly few friends, a prison record, and only fifty dollars in his pocket, he is in an extremely vulnerable position. Very often, he soon returns to prison. Prison Fellowship has developed GEO Trust, a micro-lending program designed to provide small startup loans to qualifying ex-prisoners enabling them to start small businesses. These businesses make it possible for them to succeed by providing them a means to support their families and lead productive lives within the community.

The International Center for Justice and Reconciliation is the criminal justice reform section of Prison Fellowship International. The Center helps develop restorative justice programs and does research. It works with the United Nations and local governments where possible.

The Leadership Training Institute provides a variety of specialized seminars to equip national Prison Fellowship executives and board leaders to become more effective in their management and leadership responsibilities. Leadership training courses include the Introductory Foundations for Effective Ministry and advanced sessions such as Board-Executive Leadership, Strategic Planning, and Fund Raising.

A particularly imaginative ministry is the Sycamore Tree Project, a program designed to facilitate dialogue between victims and offenders. Typically, the project brings victims into prisons to meet with "unrelated" offenders. The groups discuss together issues related to crime and its consequences.

Annually, Prison Fellowship national organizations sponsor a week of prayer for prisoners. This ministry encourages the church to pray for prisoners and participate in special outreach and support projects. The week of prayer focuses on prayer and action in support of prison chaplains, prisoners, prison officials, ex-prisoners, families, victims, and the cause of justice.

In a January 2005 fund raising letter, President Mark L. Early relates that Prison Fellowship has begun four faith-based prisons, called Inner-Change Freedom Initiative programs in Texas, Iowa, Minnesota, and Kansas. Participating inmates are given round-the-clock spiritual, educational, vocational, and life-skills training from a Christian perspective. Having worked in such a program in Arizona, I can testify that this is a very effective ministry.

In the familiar twenty-fifth chapter of the Gospel according to Matthew, Jesus clearly demonstrated that ministry to those in prison evidences genuine love for God and for those he loves. I think it is safe to say that never in the history of the world has the church been more faithful, more effective, more dedicated, or more united than it is today in ministering to those in prison, their families, and to victims of the imprisoned ones all over the world.

Trans World Radio

Continuing the metaphor of an expeditionary force waging war against evil and extending the kingdom of God into enemy territory, Trans World Radio (TWR) begun in 1952, might be called the Air Force of the Lord. Carrying through the skies the Gospel of Jesus TWR reaches beyond mountain barriers, beyond iron and bamboo curtains, beyond nations' borders that forbid the entrance of missionaries, into homes, cellars, prison cells, house churches, hospital rooms, university dormitories, wherever men live and hunger for God. "From towering cities to remote villages, TWR is being used of God to lead people from doubt to decision to discipleship."[143]

Founded by Paul Freed, its first programs were aired in February 1954, to Spain from a small transmitter in Tangier, Morocco. In only 50 years, TWR has become "the most far-reaching Christian radio network in the world." [144] It airs weekly 1800 hours of Christian programming and continually adds to the more than 180 languages and dialects in which it produces programs. Every day, from 13 superpower transmitting sites and via satellite, TWR broadcasts in more languages than Voice of America, China Radio International, BBC, and Voice of Russia combined.

TWR does not accomplish this by itself, independent of other Christian organizations. Its stated mission is "to assist the church to fulfill the command of Jesus to make disciples of all peoples and to do so by using and making available mass media." [145] In the United States alone, approximately 100 evangelical ministries team with TWR to present the message of the Gospel.[146]

Under the blessing of the Holy Spirit of God, TWR has advanced to this position, trumpeting the Gospel literally around the globe. Untold thousands have become believers, become evangelists and pastors, and gone to Heaven because of its ministry. Yet TWR not only presents the saving message of the cross of Jesus, it also speaks to the great social and physical crises of the generation in which it ministers. Its magazine, *Transworldradio,* provides the following information about these important ministries. Take note of its several ministries to the people on just one continent, Africa. "Save a Generation" is an ongoing project responsible for producing and broadcasting radio programs in three major categories: AIDS Challenge, Africa Challenge, and Generation of Hope.

These programs, while preaching the Gospel of Jesus, also teach Africans to improve their lives in practical ways. They provide a biblical foundation in matters pertaining to the family, parenting, education, business and free enterprise, agriculture, and other important topics. Experts in the medical and health fields provide important information to listeners. Unquestionably, this information has saved many lives from the ravages of diseases that can easily be prevented by good health practices.

TWR does more than send out messages into the air. It follows up its message with hands-on, "boots-on-the-ground" ministries in many forms. For example, because of the deforestation of many countries, more and more people have no wood for cooking fires. In many of these areas, TWR once provided solar-powered cookers and a corresponding broadcast that taught the people how to use these cookers. In Kenya, through involvement in a Christian orphanage and local school, TWR helps provide children with a place to live and a secular and biblical education. Another "boots-on-the-ground" ministry takes place in Cambodia. There, all persons involved in producing radio programs, the operators who record them, and their script translators are required to be involved in personal outreach among the people to whom they are ministering with their broadcasts. They not only minister over the radio to children and adults suffering with HIV/AIDS—they also serve in hospitals and orphanages where their listeners spend their last days.[147]

The March 2003 prayer letter reports on another on the ground ministry that requires a monumental amount of individual effort. Volunteers write personal responses to more than 75,000 letters received each month from Indian listeners. Many of these listeners ask for and are sent literature, Bibles, and instruction in the Word of God. It is the twenty-first-century church that is providing the money to air these life-giving broadcasts and the volunteers to answer these thousands of letters month after month.

These letters speak volumes about the effectiveness of TWR's broadcasts. Consider this: In business, a response of one percent to a radio advertisement or letter is considered good. Using this rule of thumb to evaluate how the broadcasts are being received in India, where most are illiterate and postage rates are beyond the reach of many, is extremely conservative. It is reasonable to conclude that the nearly million letters received every year indicate an attentive audience in India alone of well over a 100 million persons. Can one even estimate the incredible numbers reached daily the world over by all of TWR's 2300 three hundred stations? The huge number of listener letters say a loud "Amen" to the aforementioned quote of Campus Crusade's Bill Bright. We are certainly witnessing "the greatest spiritual harvest of all time."

TWR has two other very significant new ministries that promise to speed up the increase of the kingdom of God. The first one, known as SOTA, or Seminary of the Air, began broadcasting in early 2001. "These daily forty-five minute training programs cover critical topics such as Basic Christianity, Systematic Theology, Bible Study Methods, Christian Ethics, Evangelism and Missiology as well as Pastoral Care." [148] SOTA is aired specifically for Chinese Christians. The restrictions of the communist regime for the last fifty years have left the Chinese church with no trained or educated pastors. Each seminarian will receive personal attention and monitoring and special training sessions. Tim Klingbeil, chief development officer at TWR, describes SOTA as a special tool that the Lord has created to assist the rapidly growing church in China.

The second new ministry is similar but is directed at the world's second-largest population. India is home to over one billion people, most of whom are illiterate and poverty stricken. TWR ministers to this vast multitude in 59 different languages.[149] In January 2003, TWR, in connection with Moody Bible Institute, launched a Bible correspondence course in three languages, intending to follow up in January 2004 with three more languages. Dr. Emil Jesbasingh, regional director for TWRSouth Asia believes that "this new initiative will bring about a revolution in developing lay leaders across India by giving them fundamental Bible and theological training."[150] With the Lord's blessing on these creative and strenuous efforts, the church along with TWRIndia staff and leaders can confidently look forward to an ever-increasing harvest of souls in India in the years ahead.

The above are only a few instances of the air and ground campaign spearheaded by TWR. Only two continents were mentioned, Africa and Asia. However, it is encouraging to remember TWR is ministering to persons in all the inhabited continents in the world. It is a thrill to note that in Russia, Belarus, and Ukraine 1000 radio stations daily beam the good news of Jesus. In an April 2004 fundraising letter, President David Tucker tells of TWR's gearing up to reach the heart of Central Asia. This will air the Gospel into some of the most isolated, hard-to-reach countries on earth, including Uzbekistan, Kazakhstan, Kyrgyzstan, Tajikistan, Turkmenistan, Armenia, Azerbaijan, Georgia, Afghanistan, Chechnya, and Turkey. This nearly 2.5 million dollar investment celebrates TWR's Fiftieth Anniversary with a tremendous new advance.

In the global war for souls, evil spirits may inhabit the air (Ephesians 2:2), but they do not control the airwaves. The skies belong to the Lord of Glory and his kingdom.

InterVarsity Christian Fellowship

Intervarsity Christian Fellowship/USA (IVCF) officially began in May 1941, but its origins go back to 1877 at the University of Cambridge in England. There Christian students met together–in spite of the disapproval of some University officials–to pray, to study the Bible, and to witness to fellow students.[151] The Holy Spirit's initiative and support is evident by the fact that very soon the same thing began to happen at other colleges and universities. Eventually these groups learned of each other and formed the British InterVarsity. From the beginning, the Spirit of God planted within them a strong concern to take the Gospel to those all over the world who had never heard it.

In 1928, IVCF leapt the Atlantic when Howard Guinness, vice-chairman of the British IVCF, came to Canada in response to Canadian college students' request. In the United States in the 1930s, college students began to meet for Bible study, as their counterparts had in England nearly 50 years before. After meeting with the Canadian IVCF director, Stacey Woods, University of Michigan students formed the first IVCF chapter in the United States. In the next nine years,

IVCF/USA established 499 chapters in colleges and universities across the nation.

IVCF's mission is, "In response to God's love, grace and truth: the Purpose of IVCF Christian Fellowship/USA is to establish and advance at colleges and universities witnessing communities of students and faculty who follow Jesus as Savior and Lord: growing in love for God, God's Word, God's people of every ethnicity and culture and God's purposes in the world." [152]

There are now more than a 1000 staff serving 34,000 students and faculty. Almost 750 chapters conduct over 5,500 small group and evangelistic Bible studies. Hundreds of students become Christians every year through the witness of these students and faculty members. IVCF also sponsors mission projects in which almost 4,500 persons participate annually. In addition to their general campus ministries directed toward the entire student body, there are ministries aimed at specific targets: black campus ministries, faculty ministries, global projects, graduate ministries, international student ministries, Nurses Christian Fellowship and *Journal of Christian Nursing,* and *Student Leadership Journal.*

Perhaps the greatest achievement of IVCF is the Urbana Student Missions Conference,[153] held every three years on the campus of the University of Illinois in Urbana. In 1946, IVCF held its first Urbana Student Missions conference to call college students to come together to learn about global missions and God's will and be challenged by the world's needs. In 1954, their fourth triennial missionary convention welcomed students from 263 colleges and universities and 60 seminaries and Bible schools in the United States and Canada. Since its original conference, more than 212,000 people have attended their conferences and been challenged to participate in the great commission.

Is the twenty-first-century church dead or alive? Consider this. In addition to the millions of dollars Christians give to their local churches and to the other ministries delineated in this chapter, they donated almost 44 million dollars in 2002 to the work of IVCF. Consider also that every three years up to 35,000 young Christians pay over 2 million dollars of their own money to gather on the university campus at Urbana to contemplate the world's needs and what God would have them personally do about those needs. This one ministry of IVCF alone testifies powerfully of the vitality of the twenty-first-century church. Never in the history of the church has this sort of world missions event been consistently and regularly planned and carried out. Never have so many been so challenged to involve themselves personally in ministry to the world.

United Bible Societies

The United Bible Societies (UBS) is a world fellowship of national Bible societies. A national Bible Society is a nondenominational organization whose purpose is to translate, produce, and distribute the Christian Scriptures in languages that people can understand at prices they can afford.

The Bible Society movement is not as recent an expression of the church as most of the organizations mentioned in this chapter. Nevertheless, it bears strong testimony to the vision and vigor of the church today. The modern Bible Society movement, now active in the Netherlands, the United States, Russia and other nations, began in London in 1804, with the founding of the British and Foreign Bible Society.[154]

After World War I, the Societies began to look for ways to coordinate their work. After World War II that dream of cooperative effort became a reality. In 1946, delegates from 13 countries met at Haywards Heath, England, where the UBS was founded. Other Bible Societies were invited to join the new fellowship. By the year 2000, the UBS had grown into a family of 130 national Bible Societies, working in more than 200 countries and territories.

The wonderful cooperation of these independent national Bible Societies is making possible wide, effective, and meaningful distribution of the Holy Scriptures. People the world over who have never before had the Scriptures in any language now have them in their own mother tongue. The Scriptures are available to them at prices they can afford, regardless of the economic conditions prevailing in their country or village.

As do all of the above mentioned ministries, the Bible Societies consider themselves a resource for the church, acting as "catalysts and pioneers on the cutting edge of mission," where the local church cannot effectively minister by itself.

Although one might not associate the translation of the Scriptures with Bible Societies, in reality this is one of their most ambitious and important ministries. It is estimated that when the first Bible Society was organized there were Scriptures in fewer than 70 languages. Since then the Scriptures have been translated into well over 2000 languages. The Roman Catholic Church, anxious to provide easy access to Scripture for all its adherents, has become very active in the translation of the Scriptures. It is encouraging to note: "...of the six hundred eighty five translation projects current in 1997, one hundred seventy four have Roman Catholic involvement."

The total of all Bibles, Testaments, portions, and selections of Scriptures distributed in 2002 was over 578 million. In 2001, even more were distributed, over 633 million. Of those distributed in 2002, almost 13 million were New Reader editions. Knowing the power of God's written Word, these are very thrilling statistics. Although the report does not specify where the New Reader Scriptures were distributed, it seems likely that most went to Christians who, through the ministry of mission schools in third-world nations, are now learning to read. It is wonderful to observe how the Holy Spirit coordinates the various efforts of the church, continually enabling it to expand its healing and life-giving ministry.

Wycliffe Bible Translators And The Summer Institute Of Linguistics

As noted above, there are several groups involved in the translation of the Scriptures. Perhaps the largest and most well-known of these are Wycliffe Bible Translators and its affiliate, The Summer Institute of Linguistics. Wycliffe Bible Translators was founded in 1942 by William Cameron Townsend, a missionary to the Cakchiquel Indians of Guatemala. "Borrowing the name of the pre-Reformation hero, John Wycliffe, who first translated the Bible into English, Townsend founded 'Camp Wycliffe' in 1934 as a linguistics training school."[155] Out of this humble beginning, under the blessing of God, by 1942 two sister organizations had been organized, Wycliffe Bible Translators and The Summer Institute of Linguistics.

The first translation was completed by Wycliffe Bible Translators in 1951 in the San Miguel Mixtec language of Mexico. In the next 27 years, 99 more translations were completed. Only 23 years later, in April 2001, the five hundredth translation, a New Testament, was dedicated. Note how the Holy Spirit has been speeding up the translations of the Bible. It took nine years for the first translation, 27 years for the next 99, and only 23 to complete 400 more.

The Summer Institute of Linguistics and Wycliffe Bible Translators work together to translate Scripture, train field personnel in linguistics, and promote interest in translation. They are now working on over 1000 translations by themselves. Another 500 translations are now in progress by at least 15 other groups around the world committed to this wonderful task.

Wycliffe has 5,300 members and over 400 persons preparing to serve. Volunteers come from 55 different nations with the United States providing about 65 percent. There are now translation projects in progress in more than 70 countries and on all the continents except Antarctica. For the year ending September 30, 2002, the church of Jesus, congregations and individuals, donated to the work of Wycliffe Bible Translators over 120 million dollars.

In 1948, The Summer Institute of Linguistics and Wycliffe Bible Translators created a new organization, Jungle Aviation and Radio Service (JAARS), to assist them in their work. As Bible Translation work expanded to the Philippines, Asia, Africa and the Pacific area, JAARS[156] came along side to support the new initiatives, broadening its scope of technical service to include aviation, telecommunications, computers, construction, vernacular media, buying, shipping, and transportation services. Its international training and operating center is in Waxhaw, North Carolina.

Recognizing that some people groups may not be able to read the Bible when it is finally translated into their own mother tongue, two important programs are under way. One is literacy development and the other provides such peoples with mechanical, non-electrical means to hear the Gospel. Hand-cranked tape players are being provided to strategic persons who can play the vocalized Scriptures to non-reading listeners. The majority of people groups in the Americas now have the Scriptures in their languages, but a great many language groups in Africa, Asia, and the Pacific region are still without the Scriptures. The prophet Habakkuk saw that "The earth will be filled with the knowledge of the glory of the Lord, as the waters cover the sea."(Habakkuk 2:14) Working with partners worldwide, Wycliffe USA is accelerating the pace of Bible translation to make this vision a reality. There are 380 million people who do not yet have the Bible in their language. Wycliffe's goal is that by the year 2025 a Bible translation will be in progress for every language group that needs it. Will the goal be reached? Wycliffe USA President Bob Creson believes it will. He notes that, in the last four years, 240 new language programs were started. The previous four years saw only 100 started.[157] The 140 percent increase indicates that the speed of translations is rapidly accelerating.

However, there is more good news coming from Wycliffe Bible Translators. The Holy Spirit is doing a spectacular new thing. Wycliffe International, Youth-With-A-Mission, the International Mission Board of the Southern Baptist Convention, and Campus Crusade for Christ have jointly created an entirely new approach to reach people with the Gospel. Calling themselves Epic Partners International, they aim to involve churches everywhere to reach the 70 percent of the world's population that cannot read or prefers to hear the Gospel rather than to read it. Oral cultures communicate truth through stories, songs, proverbs, parables just as Jesus did. The Epic Partners International describe this new venture as chronological Bible storying, a technique that is being hailed as the "next wave" of mission outreach.[158] With this new approach, whole cultures and people groups can hear the Gospel in a manner consistent with their traditions without first learning to read. This new effort gives a tremendous incentive to every Bible translator, whether he is working in a hut in a mountain village or a computer laboratory at Wycliffe USA's headquarters in Orlando! It is also strong motivation to pray for the Lord's anointing on this latest assault on the kingdom of darkness by his church.

What an inspiration this gives us to ask the Lord of the Harvest to send forth "Story Tellers" into his harvest! What an encouragement to our faith it is to see the great advances the kingdom of God is making in these days!

Christian Colleges And Universities

One evidence of the vitality of the twenty-first-century church is the number and strength of the intentionally Christ-centered colleges and universities in the world, particularly in the United States and Canada.

In 1976, the Council for Christian Colleges and Universities (CCCU)[159] was created with a mission "to advance the cause of Christ-centered higher education and to help our institutions transform lives by faithfully relating scholarship and service to biblical truth." It began with 38 members and has grown in just 25 years to 105 members in North America and 64 affiliate institutions in 23 countries.

Christian higher education is thriving in North America and around the world today. In fact, growth in enrollment in Christian colleges and universities far outpaced other institutions during the reporting period (1990–1999). Statistically, according to the U.S. Department of Education National Center for Education Statistics, the growth in the colleges and universities who are members of CCCU over that period was almost 42 percent, whereas the average increase for all other college and universities was only a little over eleven percent. It is encouraging to note that nearly 184,000 students were enrolled in Christian educational institutions in the United States in 1999. That means that approximately 35,000 men and women are graduating every year from these Christ-centered schools. Having been faced with the Christian message and worldview, they are, for the most part, convinced of the validity of both.

In 2001, CCCU alumni were asked about their undergraduate education experience. Their responses indicate that most of these graduates have become active in the mission of Jesus, whatever their professions or callings. Some specific responses are noteworthy. Eighty-two percent of these graduates reported that they benefited very much from an emphasis on personal values and ethics, compared to ten percent of alumni from public institutions. Ninety percent reported that their college experience helped them develop a sense of purpose in life. Nearly all profess to be involved in church activities. They overwhelmingly affirmed that their undergraduate experience in a Christian college or university helped them connect faith with other aspects of their lives.

The Christian colleges and universities in our country are quietly and powerfully impacting the world into which their committed graduates enter, serve, and gain leadership. The Mission Statement of my Alma Mater, reads, "As a community of learners committed to historic Christianity, Roberts Wesleyan College seeks to prepare thoughtful, spiritually mature, service-oriented people who will help transform society."[160] Evidence clearly indicates that graduates from Christian colleges and universities are doing just that, "helping to transform society."

Most of these colleges and universities are direct children of the church. Like many of the great universities of our nation before them, they were started by their denominations to provide an educated clergy. Having thus begun, they have branched out into full-fledged Liberal Arts colleges and, in some instances, complete universities. All are testimonies to the church's conviction that Jesus is the Truth and that continuing in the pursuit of truth will lead to ever-greater liberty and blessing. These great educational institutions, created and largely supported by the disciples of Jesus, declare the vitality and transforming energy of the twenty-first-century church.

Focus On The Family Ministries

Focus on the Family is another ministry that by its unobtrusive and small beginning and almost miraculous increase testifies that it is a creation of the Holy Spirit for these days. When Dr. James Dobson wrote his first book, *Dare to Discipline,* did it even enter his mind that it would quickly lead to the formation of an organization that would touch the entire world? The tremendous reception given to that book evidences that people were hungry for someone with the academic credentials to stand up and say with authority, "The Bible is correct in its instructions on child rearing and family relationships." The Holy Spirit had prepared hearts all over the nation and the world to hear that word. The Holy Spirit had prepared the man who could give it to them. Like John the Baptist, he was a "man sent from God."(John 1:6)

Having read his books, listened to his radio broadcasts, and heard the shorter spots featuring Dr. Dobson, I considered myself well aware of Focus on the Family. However, when I looked into the scope of this ministry I was astounded. The following declaration was an understatement in my case. "Even those who listen regularly to our radio broadcast and have a fairly solid acquaintance with our purposes and philosophy might be surprised at the actual scope of our activities and involvement."[161] After that statement, the web site fills eleven pages with thumbnail descriptions of Focus on the Family's different ministries under six different headings: Broadcast Ministries, Online Ministries, Periodicals, Family Resources, Personal Touch Ministries, and International Outreach. These different specific ministries total 71. A few of them are briefly described here to give some idea of the variety of these ministries.

Focus on the Family Radio Broadcast

This vast radio network carrying the daily broadcast continues to expand in the number of facilities and programs offered. It is aired on nearly 2000 facilities throughout the

United States. From these daily broadcasts, fifteen-minute programs are excerpted, scripted, and translated into French, Russian, and Spanish and aired on hundreds of stations across Europe, the Commonwealth of Independent States, and Latin America.

Armed Forces Radio and Television Services Broadcast

Since 1983, the Armed Forces Radio and Television Services Network has distributed a weekly variation of the Focus on the Family daily radio program by satellite, compact disc, and shortwave radio to every U.S. military installation around the world and to all ships at sea.

Focus on Your Family's Health Broadcast

This broadcast, aired on general-market radio stations each Saturday, is hosted by Dr. Walt Larimore, a physician with more than 20 years of experience. Listeners can telephone or e-mail their questions, which Dr. Larimore answers. Connected with this broadcast is a web site that contains answers to numerous health questions, helping families increase their family's mental, spiritual, and physical health.

Focus on the Family Television Specials

Part of the original Focus on the Family film series *Where's Dad?* has been telecast over 150 times in more than 110 cities since 1984. Two episodes of *McGee And Me!* aired on ABC network nationwide and received high ratings. *Adventures in Odyssey* episodes have received airplay singularly and as a series, often in stations' Saturday morning cartoon lineup. The video *Sex, Lies, & The Truth* was released for television airings in 1993. By late 1996, this special was aired in 65 cities, including such major markets as San Francisco, Dallas, and Indianapolis. Since then, an updated program on teen sexuality and abstinence, *No Apologies,* has taken wings with significant response from stations and viewers. TV presentations on substance abuse called *Masquerade* and *Face Reality* began in 1997 and continue to air in cities throughout the country. Virtually, all current Focus on the Family television release schedules are secured on ABC, NBC, CBS, and Fox television stations. Doors have also opened for Focus on the Family programs to be aired internationally in countries such as Italy, Germany, Kenya, and even Mongolia.

Focus on the Family Periodicals

Two significant periodicals are aimed at teenagers. Breakaway Magazine for young men and Brio Magazine for young women have a combined circulation of over one-quarter of a million. These magazines show positive role models, offer sound advice on avoiding the pitfalls of adolescence, and emphasize making right choices.

Over 80,000, or about ten percent, of the physicians in the United States receive the Physician Magazine. This publication aims to help doctors strengthen their marriages in the face of intense professional pressures. It encourages them to take courageous stands on moral issues in the midst of an increasingly hostile climate and to use solid medical research to support the pro-life, pro-family cause.

Focus on the Family Ministry to Physicians

Every other year, Focus on the Family hosts a national conference for physicians in Colorado Springs. Approximately 800 physicians and their spouses from around the world attend this four-day conference.

Crisis Pregnancy Ministry

Focus on the Family assists 2,300 Crisis Pregnancy Centers and 700 other pro-life organizations across the U.S., Canada, and internationally with educational resources (booklets, videos, tapes etc.) to give to their clients. They also provide broadcasts that support their work, a biennial conference for their directors, a monthly newsletter, and a frequently updated web site.

Focus on the Family Institute

This specialized semester program of intense study launched in 1995 is offered three times a year to selected college students. They participate in classroom sessions, individual research, and internships under the leadership of family specialists. Emphasis is placed upon the integration of Judeo-Christian principles and academic disciplines. In developing this program, Focus on the Family received input from university presidents, deans, and faculty from 93 Christian colleges.

Focus on the Family Corporate Outreach

Developed to help employees respond to the stresses of family life, marital, parental, financial, or health-related problems on the job, Focus on the Family has established The Family Center in over 560 corporations and businesses across the nation, many of which are Fortune 500 companies. The CEO Forum exists to serve the needs of high-level professionals who work in a high-stress environment. This includes semiannual CEO Forums, quarterly conference calls, white papers, getaway weekends, and mentoring.

We could go on and on. There are more than 60 other unique ministries in addition to these nine that I have briefly described. These ministries are all supported by the church, which donates millions of dollars to fund the programs and then gives time and energy to do the ministry. There are few communities in the United States that are not in some way touched and enriched by the ministry of Focus on the Family. What an encouraging development this is to everyone who loves the Word of God and longs to see people everywhere benefit from its truth.

Promise Keepers

Perhaps the most recent, dynamic, worldwide ministry of the kingdom of Jesus is Promise Keepers. Started in 1990, Promise Keepers is a Christ-centered organization dedicated to introducing men to Jesus as their Savior and Lord and then helping them to grow as Christians. This is accomplished mainly through a men's conference ministry that emphasizes the Seven Promises of a Promise Keeper. The vision of Promise Keepers is simply stated: "Men Transformed Worldwide." So is their mission: "Promise Keepers is dedicated to igniting and uniting men to be passionate followers of Jesus through the effective communication of the 7 promises."[162]

In the past decade, Promise Keepers has swept across the nation like a prairie fire. Its beginnings remind one of the birth of Jesus, who slipped into the world in the nighttime, with hardly any notice. Promise Keepers began with only two men, Bill McCartney, then football coach for the University of Colorado, and Dr. Dave Wardell. At a Fellowship of Christian Athletes banquet in Pueblo, Colorado, while praying and worshipping together, Bill asked Dave, "What do you feel is the most important factor in changing a man spiritually, from immaturity to maturity?" "Discipleship" was Wardell's immediate response.[163]

McCartney then shared how there is a special dynamic when men come together to honor Jesus. He shared his vision of gathering 50,000 men at the University of Colorado's Folsom Field for training and teaching on what it means to be godly men. Thus began Promise Keepers. McCartney, Wardell, and other men of like passion began to pray and work for such a rally. In December 1990, Promise Keepers was officially incorporated in the state of Colorado. The first men's convention was held the next year with over 4,000 men attending. The next July 1,500 pastors and lay leaders gathered for the first National Leadership Conference and 22,000 men from every state in the union gathered for the second conference. During this conference, the mandate was issued for men to pursue reconciliation across racial and denominational lines.

The initial goal of 50,000 Promise Keepers to fill Folsom Field was realized at Promise Keepers in 1993. Then God expanded the vision to gather men in stadiums throughout the nation. In 1994, conferences were held in six stadiums nationwide in addition to the one in Boulder. More than 278,000 men attended these events. In 1995, in addition to 13 conferences in the United States, conferences were held in New Zealand, Australia, and Canada. Materials used in the Promise Keeper movement began to be translated into other languages. That year 738,000 men attended these conferences.

Promise Keepers continues to hold conferences across the nation annually. It has expanded its ministry to youth conferences and television and radio programs. It sponsors and provides materials for small-group Bible study and accountability groups in addition to many inspirational books for men. On October 4, 1997, Promise Keepers hosted a Sacred Assembly of men on the National Mall in Washington, D.C. An estimated one million men participated in this event, a day of personal repentance and prayer.

This dramatic movement of Christ's church has, in a dozen years, attracted over four million attendees to its rallies and many thousands of others to its small group meetings. All are challenged to commit themselves, first to Christ and then to serious discipleship and faithfulness to God and to their families and nation. Nothing like this has ever happened in the history of the world. This is certainly another strong witness to the truth of Jesus statement, "I will build my church and the gates of hell cannot resist it." (Matthew 16:18) It certainly testifies to the vitality of the present-day church and to the fact that the zeal of the Lord of Hosts has not waned.

Ministry To The World Of Islam

When considering the ministry of the twenty-first-century Church, we must not overlook the largest unreached people group in the world, the world of Islam. Millions of Muslims have either never heard of Jesus or resist him with an intensity reminiscent of the hostility faced by the Christians of the first century. Reaching this vast number of persons with the wonderful saving message of the Gospel of Jesus is probably the greatest challenge facing the church today.

Perhaps most Christians, when they think of the world of Islam, feel overwhelmed by the numbers of Muslims and by the task of reaching people with such hostility toward Jesus. However, I believe the Holy Spirit is changing that. Because of the tragic events of September 11, 2001, and the conflicts in Afghanistan and Iraq, Christians around the world have seen the faces of the Muslims in a new light. They see them as people with the same longings and needs as all other peoples of the world. They see them struggling with the bonds of a false religion. Their hearts go out to them with a new compassion. It reminds me of Jesus' response to the crowds of people who followed him everywhere he went. Matthew says, "When he saw the crowds, he had compassion on them, because they were harassed and helpless, like sheep without a shepherd. Then he said to his disciples, 'The harvest is plentiful, but the workers are few. Ask the Lord of the harvest, therefore, to send out workers into his harvest field.' " (Matthew 9:35–38)

Jesus' answer to the needs of the multitudes of harassed, helpless, and shepherdless people was prayer. One of the most encouraging evidences of the church's vitality today is that it is taking Jesus' words literally relative to the millions of Muslims. It has seen the multitudes and is asking the Lord of the Harvest to send forth laborers into his harvest field.

What has brought about this change? It appears to have been prayer. About a dozen years ago, a group of Christian leaders in the Middle East were praying for the Islamic world. "God put a burden on the hearts of these men and women to call as many Christians as possible to pray for the world of Islam." [164] In a work of the Holy Spirit that is reminiscent of Pentecost and the explosion of the church in the first century that call to prayer has been wonderfully answered. A program known as *The 30 Days Muslim Prayer Focus* was developed. It encourages Christians to pray and fast for Muslims during the 30 days of Ramadan each year. *The 30 Days Muslim Prayer Focus Prayer Guide* is now produced in more than 35 languages each year and distributed from more than 40 regional offices. According to this prayer bulletin, the number of persons participating in special prayer for the Muslims is in the tens of millions and growing steadily. Unquestionably, after having been so motivated by the Holy Spirit, when the thirty-day period is over, they continue to pray daily and earnestly for the persons enslaved in the religion of Islam.

What has been the result of this growing prayer movement for the world of Islam? God is answering this worldwide prayer effort, sending more and more missionaries and pioneering new movements. Three times as many missionaries as before are now working in the world of Islam. Rev. Robert A. Blincoe, the U.S. Director of Frontiers, credits prayer for the record number of Christians attending their missionary candidate school. He believes that the ability of the active missionaries and new Christians to continue their ministries and witness in spite of intense hostility is due to the prayers of Christian people worldwide on their behalf.[165] Many converts are now becoming missionaries themselves, often at the cost of everything they own. One such person is Sheik Barau from Uganda, a former Islamic theologian. Today he is teaching Christians in Africa to be witnesses for Christ.[166]

Campus Crusade President Douglass reports "a tremendous surge in spiritual hunger" in Iraq, possibly attributable to the showing of Mel Gibson's movie, *The Passion of The Christ*.[167] There appears to be a very strong demand for the Scriptures and as of December 2004, 250,000 Arabic New Testaments have been shipped to Iraq to supplement the 20,000 Bibles printed within Iraq.[168] In Jordan alone, 20,000 people per month are reached for Christ through Internet chatting.[169]

These beginning answers to the great prayer movement in the twenty-first-century church are definitely harbingers of wonderful things to come. "New chapters of the book of Acts are being written every day" by believers in the Middle East. [170] The vast antagonistic Muslim world, which for many loomed like a dark cloud on the horizon, now appears to be a field of ripening fruit for King Jesus. Because the hostility against Jesus is often violently expressed there will be much suffering and many martyrs, but nothing can stop the "increase of his kingdom." (Isaiah 9:7; Matthew 16:18) The zeal of the Lord Almighty expressed through his people will accomplish this.

The Modern Home School Movement

Home schooling is not totally new in the United States or the world for that matter. Long before Christian families in the 1970s became concerned about the quality of public education and the deteriorating moral conditions in many schools, a few parents taught their children at home. Persons living in isolated areas with neither the opportunity nor the money to send children to school sometimes opted to teach their children themselves. Nancy Lincoln teaching her famous son is a prime example.

However, it was not until the latter half of the twentieth century that the home school movement became a significant factor in American society. Many persons, correctly or incorrectly, came to believe that the public schools were not only failing their students, but in many instances corrupting them as well. They decided on a drastic measure. They withdrew their children from public schools and began to teach them at home. When the word spread that parents could legally and successfully do this, the practice expanded like wildfire across the nation. According to the *Gale Encyclopedia of Childhood and Adolescence,* "Home schooling is perhaps the fastest growing trend in education in this country." This agrees with the U.S. Department of Education, which says that "about five hundred thousand students or one percent of the total school age population, were taught at home in 1996."[171]

It is difficult to accurately count the number of children taught at home, but home school organizations put the estimate at almost 1.25 million. "The Department of Education's figures jumped 30% over five years, and some researchers say the number of home-schooled children is growing at about twenty five percent annually."[172] Someone reading this section may agree that the home school movement is an interesting phenomenon, but wonder why it is included in this chapter on the vitality of the church. The answer is simple. The home school movement testifies to the fact that Christians today are not only concerned about their children's education, but also totally committed to the biblical faith that they have accepted. Their faith is important enough to them that they are willing to take their children out of the public schools, where they perceive that faith to be under attack and intentionally undermined, and put forth the tremendous effort necessary to teach them at home. Again, according to *the Gale Encyclopedia of Childhood and Adolescence*, "The majority of families choose home schooling for religious reasons. About eighty percent of families who home school identify themselves as Christian."[173]

You may question my observation that the church's annual contributions of such large sums of money to evangelistic and benevolent ministries testifies to the vitality of the church. You may claim that such giving is the church's attempt to quiet its guilty conscience for its affluent lifestyle. The church will not make the effort necessary to reach the world, but will donate a few dollars to that effort. Undoubtedly, there are a few in the church with such attitudes. However, it seems to me that the home school movement indicates that the church is not as uncommitted and lazy as this criticism indicates. It is no small undertaking to teach one's children at home, particularly when the family consists of several children, including infants. It is a life-altering commitment for both parents. No longer is the mother alone all day to do the housework and prepare the meals. No longer is she free to run across the street for a coffee break with her neighbor. She is certainly not able to take on a full-time or even a part-time job to supplement the family income. She must be free to work closely with her children, plan lessons, keep abreast of state requirements, become knowledgeable about a variety of academic subjects, and perhaps negotiate issues with the school district.

Persons not fully committed to Christ are not going to make the effort required by home schooling just to pass on the Christian faith. This tremendous effort and commitment on the part of a rapidly increasing number of Christians demonstrates that the church today is willing to jump wholeheartedly into the struggle for righteousness in the world. It proves that Christians are willing to sacrifice personal gain and much leisure time to pass along their faith to the next generation. Furthermore, evidence indicates that their effort and sacrifice are paying off. Home school parents are doing their job well. "Many studies of home-schooled children demonstrated that they scored consistently better or equal to their peers in traditional schools." Furthermore, "Though there is a negative stigma attached to children who've been home-schooled, a recent University of Michigan study of home-schooled children found them to be well adjusted socially."

The ministries described in this chapter are gifts to the world from our gracious God. They express God's love for the world's peoples in very tangible ways: in the gospel—written or spoken, in food and clothing, and in face-to-face exchanges. These ministries are only a part of that which the zeal of the Lord of Hosts is doing to extend and increase Christ's kingdom. However, they are enough to encourage every believer to praise the Lord in anticipation of a great harvest of souls in the days ahead.

"I pray also that the eyes of your heart may be enlightened in order that you may know the hope to which he has called you, the riches of his glorious inheritance in the saints, and the riches of his incomparably great power for us who believe." (Ephesians 1:18–19)

Conclusion To Part I

How long have people lived on earth? No one can say for sure. Some suggest that we have been here less than 10,000 years. Others claim that we have been here for many thousands of years. We know for certain that before Jesus came life on earth was a painful, fearful, sorrowful, slavish, bloody, brief, and hopeless existence. The longer human society stretches back into antiquity, the stronger a testimony it becomes to its own inability to lift itself out of the ignorance, violence, and brutality that cursed it. Only when Jesus came did any realistic hope appear. Even so, it has been a long slow journey out of the night of ignorance and brutality. Jesus, the one who said, "I have come that they might have life, and have it to the full." (John 10:10), is the one who has been gradually lifting society out of its terrible condition. Jesus, truth and love personified, is overcoming the power of sin and its murderous children, ignorance, and brutality. It is Jesus who is bringing about the wonderful living conditions that we enjoy today. The technological discoveries that have revolutionized our lives are all from him. The astonishing medical advances that are greatly extending the length and immeasurably improving the quality of our lives are all from him. The love and respect that is given to women and children and people of all races have come directly from him. The political freedoms that a large portion of the world enjoys are all from him. Above all, he has given us a living hope for life beyond the grave by his resurrection from the dead.

How much longer will life continue on this beautiful planet before the Lord returns? How much more comfortable and wonderful will life become for us here on earth? No one knows but God himself. Clearly, Jesus has not yet finished lifting all of this world's peoples out of the darkness and bondage of sin. Ignorance and brutality are still too much with us. God has yet to reveal all the secrets hidden in creation. New ones are being discovered every day. Nor has God yet poured out upon the peoples of the world all of the blessings promised to them through Abraham's seed. Wherever the Gospel of Jesus Christ goes, the spiritual blessings and material benefits of his kingdom follow. Men and women are transformed and they change for the better the society in which they live.

These ameliorating benefits of the Gospel are just that, benefits and not the Gospel itself. Yet we need to recognize that we enjoy them because of the Gospel of Jesus. The ancient promise given to Abraham that his son would bless the entire world is certainly coming true in an ever-increasing measure, in spite of all the hatred and deception of God's enemy and ours.

We also need to recognize that these wonderful benefits and comfortable living conditions have not deterred the church from its mission. It is vigorously preaching the life-giving Gospel and tenderly ministering to the casualties of sin the world over. The church is not dying. It is not weak. It is not loafing or asleep. Perhaps best of all, it is not ineffective. Here is just one example of how God is wonderfully blessing and using his anointed church. In 1981, the Bible League printed 700 copies of the Kashinawa New Testament for 12 believers in Peru. In 2000, Wycliffe translators discovered there a thriving church of about 700 believers. Today there is a Kashinawa Bible Institute training leaders and translating the Old Testament.[174] It is tremendously encouraging to realize that never before in history has the kingdom/church been so active in carrying the Gospel to the ends of the earth and endeavoring to relieve the suffering. Just think, before 1950 there was no Campus Crusade for Christ, no World Vision, no Trans World Radio, no Prison Fellowship, no Promise Keepers, no FamilyLife conferences, and no Focus on the Family. Wycliffe Bible Translators and Summer Institute of

Linguistics were tiny organizations just beginning their ministries. InterVarsity Christian Fellowship's Urbana Missions Conferences had begun only four years earlier. Today all of these and many other groups are literally touching the entire world with evangelistic and compassionate ministries.

The origins of these fruitful organizations indicate clearly that they were raised up by the Holy Spirit. Christians can now achieve together that which no one could accomplish by himself. Churches and Christians of all denominations are giving these ministries wholehearted support.

The magazine, *Modern Reformation,* reports that donations to nineteen independent Christian missions in the United States, some of whom are mentioned in this book, totaled 1.85 billion dollars in 1999.[175] Christians have done this in addition to contributing untold millions to their local churches. Not only are Jesus' disciples sending money, they are sending their sons and daughters by the thousands to foreign fields in missionary endeavors of all kinds. The last 50 years have witnessed the greatest surge in evangelistic and compassionate ministries the world has ever seen.

One beautiful part in all this is that doors are being thrown wide open, and the kingdom of God is rushing in with the Gospel. However, even where doors remain closed, the Gospel message is going in via radio, television, and the internet. Letters by the millions from behind these walls tell of changed lives and new churches being born.

Sometimes we Christians become overwhelmed when our daily mail brings us three or four urgent requests for financial and prayer support from these mission organizations. However, these frequent appeals give us an opportunity to praise God. They witness to the truth that the church in the twenty-first century is not going on its merry way oblivious to suffering, whether the sufferers are local or on the other side of the globe. The church today is definitely not callously passing the wounded by on the other side of the road. These graphic appeals demonstrate how much the church cares and is doing to meet those needs and how the kingdom is increasing its efforts and boundaries and its blessings.

While thinking about what these appeals for funds mean, we can be encouraged by this wonderful assessment of the future by WycliffeUSA's Roy Peterson, in the 2002 Annual Report. "The needs will increase as the momentum increases and as God continues to open doors." [176]

Peterson's use of the graphic words "increase" and "momentum" underscores the truth of the ancient prophet's words, "Of the increase of his kingdom there shall be no end." (Isaiah 9:7) They indicate dynamic energy and visionary faith resident in the twenty-first-century church. William Martin, biographer of Billy Graham, concurs when he describes the church as "swelling in attendance" and "robust."[177] So do the moving words of Editor Dawn Kruger, as she writes about the future of Bible translation. "Swept along in the momentum created by the accelerated pace of Bible translation, we...see how the power of God's Word cuts new paths through resistant terrain, propelling us forward."[178]

We are witnessing Christians worldwide uniting to advance the kingdom and all of its wonderful blessings. Without discussing the reported 10,000 persons a day who are becoming Christians in the continent of Africa or the rapidly expanding numbers of underground churches in China (by unconfirmed estimates as high as forty million), it appears to this student to be irrefutable that the worldwide increase of Jesus Christ's kingdom is greater today than it has ever been in its history.

In the face of determined opposition to the Christian faith and threats of worldwide terrorism, the kingdom/church is prepared and poised for even greater advance into enemy territory. It is an exciting and fruitful time to be citizens of the kingdom of God. The fields are certainly white unto harvest and God is sending forth laborers into the harvest. To quote again Wycliffe's Dawn Kruger "The future holds tremendous possibilities as more and more people get involved. Churches are creating partnerships across the ocean. Baby Boomers are retiring early and joining forces with young adults, combining skills and experience."[179] To again quote WycliffeUSA's Peterson,

"We are beginning to see how God is able, above and beyond all we could strategize or imagine. We are experiencing unprecedented cooperation among God's people and synergistic new partnerships among national organizations, churches, denominations and ministries. We're seeing open doors around the world. We're using new technology and tools that will enable more people to participate in Bible translation and more people to receive the Word sooner. And, most important of all, we're witnessing lives changed through the Word."[180]

Although the devil will never be converted and evil will always be a powerful and destructive presence in earthly society, he has not been able nor will he ever be able to halt the progress and expansion and benefits of the Kingdom of God. "For of the increase of his government and peace there will be no end. The Zeal of the Lord Almighty will accomplish this." The future is bright for the Kingdom of God to this world's great benefit.

Jesus shall reign where'er the sun
Does his successive journeys run,
His kingdom stretch from shore to shore,
Till moons shall wax and wane no more.
Blessings abound where'er he reigns;
The prisoner leaps to lose his chains;
The weary find eternal rest,
And all the sons of want are blest.
Isaac Watts, 1719[181]

Part II

THE THEME STATED IN SCRIPTURE

High in the heavens, Eternal God,
Thy goodness in full glory shines;
Thy truth shall break through every cloud
That veils and darkens thy designs.
Life, like a fountain rich and free,
Springs from the presence of my Lord;
And in thy light our souls shall see
The glories promised in thy word.
Isaac Watts, 1719[182]

INTRODUCTION

As a preface to a more extensive look at the Scriptures, which proclaim and develop the truth of Christ's ever-increasing kingdom, Chapter One introduces this wonderful truth by briefly examining two prophecies from the Old Testament and two New Testament parables. In Chapters two through five, I discuss important Scriptures that clearly foretell the marvelous things that God will do in this world. We Christians are familiar with most of these Scriptures, but too often we do not put them together. Therefore, we miss the big picture of God's great mission in this world. Hopefully, you will be greatly encouraged by contemplating all that God has revealed to us in his inspired Word.

ONE

Two Prophecies And Two Parables

Isaiah's Prophecy Of The Continuing Increase Of Messiah's Kingdom

"Of the increase of his government and peace there will be no end. He will reign on David's throne and over his kingdom, establishing and upholding it with justice and righteousness from that time on and forever. The zeal of the Lord Almighty will accomplish this." (Isaiah 9:7)

Standing in the shadow of verse six, one of the most magnificent mountain peaks of praise to the Son of God in the Old Testament, this verse seems to have been overlooked by most Christians. Its truth, however, is the message of this book.

Notice the promise: "There shall be no end of the *increase*[183] of Christ's government and peace." This is a much more exciting prophecy than one that simply says his kingdom will never end. This prophecy says his kingdom and his peace will keep on increasing from henceforth, even forever. In spite of all opposition, his kingdom will increase and impact the world in which we live.

The Hebrew word *marbiyth,* here translated "increase," comes from the root word *rabah,* which means to increase (in whatever respect), continue, enlarge, excel, exceed, to be full of, grow up, heap, increase, have more in number. According to the revelation given to Isaiah, Christ's kingdom is not going to be insignificant in this world. It will fill the earth with the king's glory.

Christ will reign on David's throne and over his kingdom, establishing and upholding it with justice and righteousness from that time on and forever. Jesus told Governor Pilate, "My kingdom is not of this world." (John 18:36) His kingdom is not of this world, but the citizens of the kingdom of God are still "in this world." The more the kingdom of God increases, the more the transformed subjects of the invisible kingdom will transform the visible world. A good illustration of the redeeming impact upon society is the influence that secular historians credit to the Wesleyan Revival in eighteenth century England. J. H. Plumb claims, "It is not too much to say that without the influence which the Whitfield-Wesley revivals had at the grass roots, it is doubtful whether England would have avoided its own version of the French Revolution."[184] Jesus said that Christians are the "salt of the earth." (Matthew 5:13) There was less than one Christian among every fifty persons in England, yet their "salty" presence so elevated the condition of the common man that England was saved from the bloody rampages and ravages that France experienced.

"The zeal of the Lord Almighty will accomplish this." (Isaiah 9:7) Isaiah saw that the increase of the kingdom of God was not dependent upon the efforts of the kingdom's subjects or the world's cooperation. The zeal of the Lord Almighty will make it happen. Consequently, the kingdom's increase is a certainty. Isaiah's affirmation is as confident as

Jesus' words to the disciples, "I will build my church, and the gates of Hades will not overcome it." (Matthew 16:18) The ancient prophet's encouraging words are coming true in our world today. In spite of fierce opposition, Christ's kingdom is expanding more rapidly than ever before on ever-widening fronts. The gates of Hades have not been able to stop or slow it or prevent the increasing momentum. We saw in the last chapter of Part I the imaginative and creative ways in which the Holy Spirit is expanding the kingdom of God. Clearly, the zealous Lord Almighty is empowering this increase.

Daniel's Prophecy Concerning Nebuchadnezzar's Dream

"You looked, O king, and there before you stood a large statue—an enormous, dazzling statue, awesome in appearance. The head of the statue was made of pure gold, its chest and arms of silver, its belly and thighs of bronze, its legs of iron, its feet partly of iron and partly of baked clay. While you were watching a rock was cut out, but not by human hands. It struck the statue on its feet of iron and clay and smashed them. Then the iron, the clay, the bronze, the silver and the gold were broken to pieces at the same time and became like chaff on a threshing floor in the summer. The wind swept them away without leaving a trace. But the rock that struck the statue became a huge mountain and filled the whole earth.

In the time of those kings, the God of heaven will set up a kingdom that will never be destroyed, nor will it be left to another people. It will crush all those kingdoms and bring them to an end, but it will itself endure forever. This is the meaning of the vision of the rock cut out of a mountain, but not by human hands, a rock that broke the iron, the bronze, the clay, the silver and the gold to pieces. The great God has shown the king what will take place in the future. The dream is true and the interpretation is trustworthy." (Daniel 2:31–35, 44–45)

With gracious wisdom and sovereignty, our great God chose to make known to the proud, heathen king Nebuchadnezzar the divine purpose for the world and the ultimate glory of God's eternal kingdom. This is an inspiring revelation about the kingdom that the God of Heaven will establish.

The reference to a rock being cut out of the mountain, but not by human hands, tells us that God himself will establish this kingdom. Significantly, God gives believers the opportunity to participate in kingdom-building and expansion, but its future is not dependent upon them. Jesus emphasized this same truth in his statement: "...I will build my church, and the gates of Hades will not overcome it." (Matthew 16:18) The kingdom is God's idea, God's program, and God's work. He will bring it to completion. Regardless of how God's kingdom may appear at a particular time in history–either weak or strong–the ultimate success of the kingdom is never in doubt.

Daniel saw that "...the rock that struck the statue became a huge mountain and filled the whole earth."(Daniel 2:35) The kingdom of God will fill the earth. Isaiah proclaimed this same principle of growth: "Of the increase of His kingdom and Peace there shall be no end." (Isaiah 9:7) The kingdom will not remain a tiny, insignificant body in this great world. It will fill the earth. It may not yet have done so, but it is going to do so.

Daniel saw that the kingdom would crush all other kingdoms of the world so that nothing will remain of them. We are not accustomed to using such violent terms to describe the impact of the kingdom upon the worldly societies in which it is planted. Yet Jesus taught this exact truth in his kingdom parables, using less violent terms. In fact, Daniel's prophecy foreshadows Jesus' command to his dozen or so disciples just prior to his Ascension, "Go into all the world and make disciples of all nations." (Matthew 28:19) The nonviolent kingdom of peace and love will transform the whole earth, bringing down the seemingly all-powerful kingdoms of hatred and selfishness. What an amazing and thrilling paradox!

Can you imagine how ironic, yet how inspiring, Daniel's interpretation of Nebuchadnezzar's dream might have seemed to the Apostle Paul, if he pondered it while chained in Roman prisons? Love's victory over violence is reflected in his encouragement to that tiny sprout of the kingdom in Corinth:

"Though we live in the world, we do not wage war as the world does. The weapons we fight with are not the weapons of the world. On the contrary, they have divine power to demolish strongholds. We demolish arguments and every pretension that sets itself up against the knowledge of God, and we take captive every thought to make it obedient to Christ." (2 Corinthians 10:3)

Jesus' Parable Of The Mustard Seed

"The kingdom of heaven is like a mustard seed, which a man took and planted in his field. Though it is the smallest of all your seeds, yet when it grows, it is the largest of garden plants and becomes a tree, so that the birds of the air come and perch in its branches." (Matthew 13:31–32, see also Mark 4:32, Luke 13:18–19)

Considering the small number of disciples Jesus left behind when he ascended into Heaven, it is easy to see why he likened the kingdom to a mustard seed. This seed is the smallest of the seeds his listeners commonly planted in their gardens, but the size of the seed is not the significant thing in the parable. The life in the seed and the ultimate size of the plant that would grow from that tiny seed are the truly important truths. Jesus said that it would eventually become the largest of the garden plants, actually a tree.

It is true that the early visible expression of Jesus' kingdom was a very small one. It is just as true that the visible expression of the same kingdom is now a very large one. "In 1492 less than 20 percent of the world's population was Christian. Out of that Christian population, the vast majority, over 90% lived in what eventually became Europe." [185] Now, according to Chidester, "Five centuries after Columbus, roughly one-third of the world's population subscribes to Christianity."[186] It is not yet the largest plant in the garden of the world, but with the steady growth of a plant in the garden, it is becoming so. It is the tree the Lord has planted. It will eventually become the giant tree the Lord has promised.

As demonstrated in the last chapter of Part I, the King is dramatically increasing his kingdom all over the world. The gates of Hades everywhere in the world are under siege by Spirit-anointed kingdom members.

Jesus' Parable Of The Yeast

"The kingdom of heaven is like yeast that a woman took and mixed into a large amount of flour until it worked all through the dough." (Matthew 13:33, see also Luke 13:18–21)

Here our Lord speaks directly of the increasing and pervasive influence of the kingdom of God upon the society that it invaded. Note that Jesus says the yeast will eventually work its way all through the dough. The kingdom will eventually impact the entire world. When one considers the chemical impact that yeast makes upon every part of the flour into which it is placed, he realizes that the pervasive impact of the kingdom upon the world will not be superficial, but deep and profound. Energy from within (the love of God resident in his believing children) changes the composition, behavior, appearance, and flavor of the whole of the world's society.

There is a significantly different emphasis in these two parables we are considering. The parable of the mustard seed indicates how vast the kingdom will become. The parable of the yeast indicates how every aspect of society will be touched and transformed by God's kingdom.

As a child in rural New York, I was always fascinated by the bread-making process of my mother and grandmother. The yeast was broken up and mixed by hand into the dough. Then the hidden yeast and the mixed-up dough were placed in a large pan above the warming oven of the old wood stove. At first, nothing appeared to be happening. After some considerable time, the dish towel covering the pan began to lift up, very slowly at first, but more rapidly as the whole mass swelled. Had not Mother removed the pan and brought it back to the mixing board, the rapidly swelling dough would have overflowed the pan and spilled down onto the stove.

Looking back over the 2000-plus years of the history of the world since the birth of Christ, one can see an exact parallel and perfect expression of the prediction in the Lord's parable. Jesus' kingdom took many years to make its powerful world-transforming presence known. At first, it was an illegal hidden presence in the powerful Roman Empire, but the covering of darkness is gradually lifting. The kingdom is more rapidly increasing. Its impact upon the world is becoming more obvious and significant. It is all happening from within, without guns, marching armies, political pressure, or external force of any kind.

In an ancient prophecy of Isaiah, which the Holy Spirit applied to King Jesus (Matthew 12:18–20), we see how this leaven—the kingdom of God—will effectively change society for the better, not by outside coercion and government regulation, but from within.

"Here is my servant whom I uphold, my chosen one in whom I delight. I will put my Spirit on him, and he will bring justice to the nations. He will not shout or cry out, or raise his voice in the streets. A bruised reed he will not break and a smoldering wick he will not snuff out. In faithfulness he will bring forth justice; he will not falter or be discouraged till he establishes justice on the earth. In his law the islands will put their hope." (Isaiah 42:1–4)

After considering these four graphic Scriptures, one must conclude, whenever he might live in history and however bleak the situation might appear to be, better days are ahead. It should comfort every Christian to know that his ministry is not in vain, however difficult the work may be or however fruitless his labors may seem. God's kingdom will continually increase until the societies of the entire world have been wonderfully transformed to the glory of our Kinsman Redeemer King.

"It might seem incredible that the humble ministry of this obscure Galilean could be the dawning of the new age of God. Yet it is! What has been begun here will surely go on to its conclusion; nothing can stop it."[187] Trueblood reminds us: "Christ's aim was not to produce a little sect, which would have been comparatively easy, but to change the entire human enterprise."[188] John Stott considers the metaphors used by God in his conversation with Abraham about his descendants to be indicative of the vastness of God's future plans. He notes that these metaphors, "stars in the sky" and "sand on the seashore" (Genesis 22:17) symbolize numberlessness. He sees this vast numberless multitude of blessed ones also symbolized by the multitudes "...from every nation, tribe, people and language . . ." (Revelation 7) standing before God's throne. Stott rejoices "...that the missionary labours of the church will come to such a glorious and God-honouring climax."[189]

Two

God's Revelation Through The Ancients

Noah

Noah had been shut up in the ark for a long time, over 230 days. The glorious rainbow that greeted him and his family when they came out of the ark was not an optic shock occasioned by the sudden impact of light upon eyes accustomed to darkness by long months of confinement in the pitch-coated ark. God set the rainbow in the sky as a sign of the everlasting covenant he was establishing between himself and living creatures of every kind on the earth. "Never again will all life be cut off by the waters of a flood. Never again will there be a flood to destroy the earth." (Genesis 9:11)

Noah certainly did not take this covenant at anything more than its face value nor see in it the promise of a divinely established kingdom whose increase would never end. However, we, who know all about the advent and work of Jesus, can see that in this covenant God gave a hint of another plan for dealing with the evil in men's hearts and the consequent violence on earth. Instead of threatening to destroy all life on earth a second time, he suggested that he had another plan. His intention to redeem mankind and consequently redeem and bless society would be spelled out in more detail later.

Abraham

"The Lord had said to Abram, 'Leave your country, your people and your father's household and go to the land I will show you. I will make you into a great nation and I will bless you; I will make your name great, and you will be a blessing. I will bless those who bless you, and whoever curses you I will curse; and all peoples on earth will be blessed through you.'" (Genesis 12:1–3)

The Lord was much more specific with Abraham than he had been with Noah. God told Abraham plainly, "… all peoples on earth will be blessed through you." (v.3)

The blessing of the Lord given to an individual, family, or nation was taken very seriously by the ancients. They sought such pronounced blessings. We can be very sure Abraham understood that the Lord intended to make a significant positive difference in the lives of all peoples on earth through him. Two more times in the following years, the Lord appeared to Abraham and reiterated his promise: "Look up at the heavens and count the stars, if indeed you can count them. So shall your offspring be." (Genesis 15:5) And in Genesis 22:18: "Your descendants will take possession of the cities of their enemies, and through your offspring all nations on earth will be blessed."

God did not reveal to Abraham everything he was going to do. One thing, however, God did make clear: His blessed ministry to the world through Abraham was not to be a small thing. The magnitude of God's intended ministry though the patriarch must have been one of the strongest motives Abraham had to go from his home in Babylon and to obey God so implicitly throughout his whole life. Abraham was an idol worshipper in Ancient Babylon. He was persuaded by the one true God to leave his idols and his homeland and launch out in faith because this living God promised to bless the entire world through him. Cannot we, who have in Jesus the much fuller revelation of God's great purposes, lift up our eyes in anticipation and labor with joy and faith? We certainly can, knowing that those promised blessings are indeed coming to all the world. (1 Corinthians 15:58)

"It is no exaggeration to say that Genesis 12:1–4 is the most unifying text of the whole Bible…The rest of the Bible is an unfolding of it, and subsequent history has been a fulfillment of it."[190] Stott claims that "The tragedy of the Old Testament is that Israel kept forgetting the universal scope of God's promise."[191] Tragically, many in the modern church seem to have forgotten not only the universal scope of God's promises but also his power to bring them to pass. Having forgotten his promises, they overlook what he has already done and what he is doing now. Instead of living with vibrant enthusiasm and confidence, they live in pessimism, decrying how bad things are becoming.

Jacob

To the heel-grasper, the conniver known as Jacob, God said, "…your name will be Israel." (Genesis 35:10) Israel means "Prince of God." Then God gave him a gracious promise. "I am God Almighty; be fruitful and increase in number. A nation and a community of nations will come from you, and kings will come from your body." (Genesis 35:11)

Here again, God reveals his intentions, expanding on the promise he had given to Abraham. To Abraham, he had said, "I will make you into a great nation." To Jacob he added, "A community of nations will come from you." When the Apostle Paul wrote to the gentile Christians in Galatia, "Now you, brothers, like Isaac, are children of promise." (Galatians 4:28) He was certainly claiming that they were part of God's believing family and kingdom. He claimed that they were the true children of Abraham, Isaac, and Jacob.

Just how much of God's gracious and great intentions Jacob understood is, of course, unknown. However, in the blessing he gave his son Judah, he expressed the power that was resident in God's blessing on Abraham's descendants and the extent to which they would influence the world. "The scepter will not depart from Judah, nor the ruler's staff from between his feet, until he comes to whom it belongs, and the obedience of the nations is his." (Genesis 49:10) This is a direct reference to the coming Messiah King.

The Lord does not speak of Judah's descendants or his kingdom as being pushed around and defeated, nor should we. He pictures his kingdom as full of glory in the world, something to be taken into consideration in the affairs of men and actually triumphant over all opposition. This was the view of the early church, so wonderfully expressed by the Apostle Paul. He reminds us that although the weapons of the church's struggles and triumph are not the world's weapons, "…they have divine power to demolish strongholds and every pretension that sets itself up against the knowledge of God and take captive every thought and make it obedient to Christ." (2 Corinthians 10:4–5)

Balaam

As evil as he was eloquent, Balaam seems a strange person for the Lord to choose as spokesman for some of the most beautiful and significant revelations of his unchangeable plans. Yet God showed us through Balaam's oracles several very significant features of his plan for the ages. Each one is thrilling in its picture of the Lord's loving, well-thought-out plan. Spoken to Balak, Israel's avowed enemy, Balaam's second oracle contains the most revealed information on the subject of our particular inquiry.

"Arise, Balak and listen; hear me, son of Zippor. God is not man, that he should lie, nor a son of man, that he should change his mind. Does he speak and then not act? Does he promise and not fulfill? I have received a command to bless; he has blessed and I cannot change it. No misfortune is seen in Jacob, no misery observed in Israel. The Lord their God is with them; the shout of the King is among them. God brought them out of Egypt; they have the strength of a wild ox. There is no sorcery against Jacob, no divination against Israel. It will now be said of Jacob and of Israel, 'See what God has done!' The people rise like a lioness; they rouse themselves like a lion that does not rest till he devours his prey and drinks the blood of his victims." (Numbers 23:18–24)

Several truths are revealed to us in this beautiful oracle. The future success of Israel is assured because of God's faithfulness to his promised word. God will be their king. He will be among them in his almighty power. Nothing can stop them. No spiritual adversary will have any power against them. Their enemies will be devoured in a total triumph. The unchangeable God has unchangeable plans for his people. No matter the opposition, whether a king in ancient times or a political activist in modern times, he will not succeed in preventing the increase of God's kingdom.

In the beautiful fourth oracle (Numbers 24:15–19), the Lord tells us "A star will come out of Jacob; a scepter will rise out of Israel."(v.17) "Edom will be conquered; Seir his enemy, will be conquered, but Israel will grow strong. A ruler will come out of Jacob and destroy the survivors of the city." (vv. 18–19)

Matthew Henry sees this obvious reference to the Messiah's kingdom as a testimony that his kingdom shall be universal and victorious over all opposition. "Christ shall be king, not only of Jacob and Israel, but of all the world."[192]

Jacob spoke of the scepter arising out of Israel. We can see in this beautiful vision the star of Messiah's kingdom gradually ascending in the sky, three thousand years after Balaam uttered that wonderfully simple promise.

In the next oracle, Amalek is introduced. (Numbers 24:20) A descendant of Esau, Amalek was an avowed and constant enemy of Israel as they made their way through the wilderness. He is a picture of our constant archenemy, Satan, whose antipathy toward the Savior is expressed in constant attacks upon us as we endeavor to follow Christ.

In Exodus 17, there is an account of a tremendous battle that occurred at Rephidim when the Amalekites attacked Israel. Israel was victorious only because Moses held his hands up to the Lord. When the battle was over, the Lord said to Moses, "Write this on a scroll as something to be remembered and make sure Joshua hears it, because I will completely blot out the memory of Amalek from under heaven." (Exodus 17:14) Then Moses built an altar and called it "The Lord is my Banner," saying "For hands were lifted up to the throne of the Lord. The Lord will be at war against the Amalekites from generation to generation." (v. 15)

This was written to direct Israel never to make any league with the Amalekites.[193] In Balaam's fourth oracle, the Lord makes clear that the Amalekites are never going to triumph, but rather, Amalek and his tribe will come to ruin at last.

It doesn't appear to me that there is ever going to be a time when it can be correctly said, "We are now in a 'Post Christian Era.'" On the contrary, the visions given to Baalim and the promises made to Abraham, Isaac, and Jacob cause me to expect an ever-greater increase in God's kingdom.

Moses

At the end of his long and arduous ministry to the children of Israel, just before turning over the leadership of God's people to Joshua, Moses spoke to Israel in the desert by the Jordan. He rehearsed the ups and downs of their relationship to the Lord and God's faithfulness to them. Then Moses encouraged them to trust in the Lord, to cross the Jordan, and drive out the inhabitants of the Promised Land. He says, "You may say to yourselves, 'These nations are stronger than we are. How can we drive them out?' But do not be afraid of them; remember well what the LORD your God did to Pharaoh, and to all Egypt." (Deuteronomy 7:17–18)

Moses standing there in the desert talking to Jacob's children reminds me of Jesus standing on the Mount of Ascension speaking to the children of his heavenly Father. The message Moses gave his audience is essentially the message Jesus told his twelve disciples.

"Do not be terrified by them, for the LORD your God, who is among you, is a great and awesome God. The LORD your God will drive out those nations before you, little by little...The Lord your God will deliver them over to you, throwing them into great confusion until they are destroyed. He will give their kings into your hand, and you will wipe out their names from under heaven. No one will be able to stand against you; you will destroy them." (Deuteronomy 7:21–24)

Moses' words, "The LORD your God, who is among you," (v.21) remind us of the words Jesus spoke to his small band of disciples, "Lo, I am with you always, even to the end of the age." (Matthew 28:20)

What a difference there is between Moses speaking to that great multitude of Israelites, perhaps two million persons, and Jesus speaking to his dozen disciples. If the Israelites felt hesitant in the face of their adversaries, how must those few disciples have felt when they heard Jesus speak? "Go and make disciples of all nations, baptizing them in the name of the Father and of the Son and of the Holy Spirit and teaching them to obey everything I have commanded you." (Matthew 28:19) If any people ever felt small and insignificant in the face of an incredible challenge, it must have been those few disciples.

God did for Israel exactly as he promised. He enabled Israel to overcome the stronger inhabitants and take over the Promised Land. We see a parallel in the Book of the Acts of the Apostles. God enabled the early church to spread across the entire Roman Empire in a matter of only a few years. The same thing is happening today as the kingdom of God engages the world with its message of love and grace. While the above verses in Deuteronomy may not be prophecy, they are certainly a true picture of the victory that Christ is giving the kingdom of God. Let us take great courage from that fact.

On this passage in Deuteronomy, Henry writes "We must not think that because the deliverance of the church and the destruction of its enemies are not effected immediately, therefore they will never be effected."[194] Evil is still a powerful force in our society, but I believe that those who think that the Lord's enemies are gaining ground are mistaken. Nevertheless, we must remember that it may take some considerable time yet before the full extent of the prophesied kingdom's expansion and impact are achieved.

Before we leave this event, we should note the words of Moses:

"The LORD did not set his affection on you and choose you because you were more numerous than other peoples, for you were the fewest of all peoples. But it was because the LORD loved you and kept the oath he swore to your forefathers that he brought you out with a mighty hand and redeemed you from the land of slavery, from the power of Pharaoh king of Egypt. Know therefore that the LORD your God is God; he is the faithful God, keeping his covenant of love to a thousand generations of those who love him and keep his commands. But those who hate him he will repay to their face by destruction . . ." (Deuteronomy 7:7–10)

We have seen how God spoke to Abraham in Babylon, promising great blessings to the world through his seed. Through Moses' words, God reminds the Israelites (and us) that He has not forgotten his promise to their (and our) father. He is a faithful God. Thousands of generations of believers will find him so. So will those who hate him. They will not overcome. They will be destroyed.

Moses ends his final word to the people he has loved and served for so many years with a blessing on the tribes of Israel. That great blessing concludes with these words: "Blessed are you, O Israel! Who is like you, a people saved by the LORD? He is your shield and helper and your glorious sword. Your enemies will cower before you, and you will trample down their high places." (Deuteronomy 33:29)

How symbolic are Moses' words of the victory of the true Israel in this world! "What is here said of the church of Israel is certainly to be applied to the church of the firstborn."[195] The apostle Paul calls the church the Israel of God. (Galatians 6:16) So Christian believers, the true children of Israel, have great assurance of a wonderful victory over all of the Lord's and our own spiritual enemies. Moses tells us that our enemies will cower before us, and we will trample down their high places.

With such great blessings as these resting upon the church, should we not proceed with our witness and work in great confidence? God's purpose will succeed and his name will be ultimately glorified. This is no time to be pessimistic. There will never be such a time. When Jesus returns he will gather his worldwide triumphant church to himself and bring judgment on all the remainder. "Look, he is coming with the clouds, and every eye will see him, even those who pierced him: and all the peoples of the earth will mourn because of him. So shall it be! Amen." (Revelation 1:7)

The Judges

While Scripture pictures the kingdom of God triumphant over evil, it never indicates that evil will be eradicated from the earth before the return of Christ.

The Book of Judges is largely the record of the tribes of Israel and their erratic relationship with the Lord. As long as Israel carefully worshiped and served the Lord wholeheartedly, he protected and prospered them in their territories. However, their faithfulness seemed to last only as long as their leaders. When their leaders went the way of all flesh, Israel lapsed into idol worship and unfaithfulness to the Lord. To discipline them, God allowed their unconquered neighbors to overwhelm them and enslave them. When they suffered greatly and called upon him, God, in his mercy and grace, would raise up a judge to deliver them. Then, as before, they would go back to rebellion. Chapter 2 of Judges rehearses Israel's behavior and introduces the themes of the book. At the end of chapter 2, the Lord made an announcement that has had relevance to the kingdom of God throughout its history:

"Because this nation has violated the covenant that I laid down for their forefathers and has not listened to me, I will no longer drive out before them any of the nations Joshua left when he died. I will use them to test Israel and see whether they will keep the way of the LORD and walk in it as their forefathers did." (Judges 2:20–22)

Clearly, evil will be with us to the very end of the age. Just as the wind strengthens the root systems of trees, God has said that he will use evil opposition to test and strengthen his people. Throughout history, whenever God's people have been careless and faithless, they, like Israel during the times of the judges and the kings, have suffered at the hands of their unbelieving enemies. Time and again, God has used those same enemies to cause his people to fall on their knees and repent of their sins and return to their heavenly Father. Furthermore, in times when the church was the most faithful and effective in its witness, the enemy roused itself in vigorous unsuccessful attacks upon the kingdom of God. Many interpret the hostile attitude of unbelieving peoples around us today as indication that the church has failed and that we have moved beyond the Christian era. A dead church arouses no opposition. I believe the hostility of the anti-Christ forces today evidences the success of the kingdom of God, not its failure. The church is no longer the quiet, peaceful, passive body that it seemed to be for several decades. It has roused itself and is moving very effectively into every area of society, irritating and possibly even frightening the opposition. Conversely, God uses the opposition to strengthen the spiritual vitality of his people. He has always done so, just as in Judges he indicated he would.

THREE

God's Revelation Through David

King and Psalmist of Israel, David was used by our gracious God to reveal more of God's personal beauty and glorious plan for the future of his people and world than any other Old Testament personality. David was, as he himself tells us, "…the man exalted by the Most High, the man anointed by the God of Jacob, Israel's singer of songs." (2 Samuel 23:1)

This unlikely son of Jesse, throughout years of suffering and humiliation and years of power and glory, penned some of the most beautiful praises ever written and painted for us some of the loveliest pictures eyes have ever been privileged to look upon. By the inspiration of the Holy Spirit, he revealed to us scenes and mysteries known previously only by God.

The Victories And The Expansion Of Christ's Kingdom In This World

In one of his most beautiful songs, sung to the Lord,

who had delivered him from the hand of all his enemies and from the hand of Saul, he wrote:

"You have delivered me from the attacks of my people; you have preserved me as the head of nations. People I did not know are subject to me, and foreigners come cringing to me; as soon as they hear me they obey me. They all lose heart; they come trembling from their strongholds...Therefore I will praise you, O Lord among the nations. I will sing praises to your name. He gives his king great victories; he shows unfailing kindness to his anointed, to David and his descendants forever." (2 Samuel 22:44–45,50–51)

When we consider that David was the most graphic Old Testament picture of the Messiah, the Lord Jesus, these inspired verses take on tremendous significance for our day. They picture vividly the victories of the Messiah's kingdom and its spread over the entire world. There is no hint that the king will tire or the kingdom will expend all its energy and resources, eventually losing out to the opposition. These prophecies speak rather of the opposition coming out of its strongholds, trembling in total defeat and yielding total obedience to Christ. They speak of God's unfailing kindness to David's descendants forever. While time lasts, David never foresees a time which would be a "Post-Christian era."

The Book of Psalms is rich with songs and promises of the worldwide expansion of Messiah's kingdom. We can select only the most obvious ones, or we would never reach the end of this book.

In the short and vivid Psalm 2, David, by the Holy Spirit, expresses two themes to which he returns again and again in the larger Book of Psalms. First, after describing the widespread and total opposition that our loving God and the Lord Jesus have faced in this world, David reveals the absolute disregard God has for the strength, vows, and hostility of his enemies: "The One enthroned in heaven laughs; the Lord scoffs at them." God says, "I have installed my King on Zion, my holy hill," (vv. 4–5) as if to say, "What are you going to do about it?" In this vibrant interchange, the Holy Spirit reveals and forecasts for us the absolute, total victory of God over all his opposition in this world.

Second, he reveals again the extent and breadth of Messiah's future kingdom: "I will proclaim the decree of the Lord. He said to me, 'You are my Son, today I have become your Father. Ask of me, and I will make the nations your inheritance, the ends of the earth your possession.'" (vv.7–8)

The Messiah's kingdom will not be a weak little territory on the edge of the Mediterranean Sea. Rather, it will grow in power, encircle the globe, eventually reaching to the ends of the earth. These two truths are proclaimed in many other places in the Psalms. Consider how the following verses from various Psalms reveal the worldwide extension of the kingdom of God. They are explicit about the Messiah's authority and the extent of his kingdom.

"All the ends of the earth will remember and turn to the Lord, and all the families of the nations will bow down before him, for dominion belongs to the Lord and he rules over the nations." (Psalm 22: 27–28)

"Gird your sword upon your side, mighty one; clothe yourself with splendor and majesty. In your majesty ride forth victoriously in behalf of truth, humility and righteousness; let your right hand display awesome deeds. Let your sharp arrows pierce the hearts of the king's enemies; let the nations fall beneath your feet." (Psalm 45:3–5)

"Be still and know that I am God; I will be exalted among the nations, I will be exalted in the earth." (Psalm 46:10)

"Clap your hands, all you nations; shout to God with cries of joy. How awesome is the LORD Most High, the great King over all the earth! He subdued nations under us, peoples under our feet." (Psalm 47:1–3)

"God is the King of all the earth; sing to him a psalm of praise. God reigns over the nations; God is seated on his holy throne. The nobles of the nations assemble as the people of the God of Abraham, for the kings of the earth belong to God; he is greatly exalted." (Psalm 47:7–9)

"He will rule from sea to sea and from the River to the ends of the earth. The kings of Tarshish and of distant shores will bring tribute to him;…All kings will bow down to him and all nations will serve him." (Psalm 72:8,10–11)

These Scriptures agree on the ultimate success and advance of the kingdom. Certainly David had no idea of the size of the earth, but he knew how great God was. He knew the God of Israel was the creator and ruler of the entire earth, not just a tribal deity. Through the Holy Spirit's inspiration, he knew and revealed to us the universal character of the realm of the king of Glory. David concludes Psalm 72 with this prophetic prayer: "Praise be to his glorious name forever; may the whole earth be filled with his glory. Amen and Amen." (v. 19) Does not this simple prayer remind you of the second petition in the Lord's Prayer? "Your kingdom come, your will be done on earth as it is in heaven." (Matthew 6:10) Is it not, in fact, the same prayer?

Obviously, at the end of the age, God will be glorified by all men and nations. Every knee will bow and confess Jesus is Lord to the glory of God the Father. We need to recognize, however, the contexts of David's prophecies indicate clearly that God's great power and glory will be seen and honored in this world, not just at the judgment. We do have a wonderful future in eternity. There is no question about that. Tragically, the truth revealed to the inspired prophets of the Old Testament has been overlooked. They envisioned the Lord gradually extending his kingdom to the ends of the earth and filling the earth with his glory. Israel saw her God as the Lord of history, working his purpose in history and calling Israel to serve that purpose. "She could conceive no other end for history than the victorious establishment of God's people under that rule."[196]

This victorious establishment is "to have its full accomplishment in the days of the Messiah." [197] The world-wide adoration of the Messiah will be a historical reality, not just one in eternity. Bright maintains, "The New Testament announces with one voice and with unshakable assurance, that all the hope of Israel has become present fact in Jesus." [198] Further, "It lies at the very heart of the gospel message to affirm that the Kingdom of God has in a real sense become present fact, here and now."[199] These truths certainly agree with Isaiah's insistence upon the Lord's intention and ability to continually increase his kingdom.

Psalm 110 paints a delightful picture reminiscent of David's description in Psalm 2 of the Almighty on his throne, listening to the tumult, the raging and ranting of his enemies, and laughing. Here we see him turning to his son, the Messiah, and saying, "Sit at my right hand until I make your enemies a footstool for your feet. The LORD will extend your mighty scepter from Zion; you will rule in the midst of your enemies." (vv.1–2)

In Psalm 2, God declares that all this is certain by his eternal decree. Here, David says, "The Lord has sworn and will not change his mind. The Lord is at your right hand; he will crush kings on the day of his wrath. He will judge the nations, heaping up the dead and crushing the rulers of the whole earth. (vv. 4–6) We have learned from history that it is a slow process. Nevertheless, Scripture assures us, God will be glorified on earth. Christ will be exalted to the throne of an eternal and increasing kingdom in which all his enemies will be subjected to his will, "rendered infallibly certain by the word and oath of the Almighty God."[200] We, who live such short lives, want to see everything come to fulfillment in our lifetime. It should encourage us to remember that God has no such constraints as a life span of threescore and ten.

He does not have to accomplish everything in such a short time.

In Psalm 132:11–18 we can readily see the prophetic expansion and blessed union of Christ's kingdom and church spoken of in the preface.

"The Lord swore an oath to David, a sure oath that he will not revoke: 'One of your own descendants I will place on your throne…The LORD has chosen Zion, he has desired it for his dwelling: This is my resting place forever and ever; here I will sit enthroned, for I have desired it…Here I will make a horn grow for David and set up a lamp for my anointed one. I will clothe his enemies with shame, but the crown on his head will be resplendent.' "

"The promises concerning Zion's hill are as applicable to the gospel-church as these concerning David's seed are to Christ."[201] This passage makes it clear that the increase of the kingdom/church must occur during the history of the world, not after the end of time. It will happen. The psalmist repeatedly emphasizes that no opposition can stop the increase of his kingdom, no matter how well organized, financed, or fierce. History has proved it so. Rome could not stop it. The Holy Roman Empire could not. Unbelieving philosophers, thinkers, and kings have not been able to. The Deists and Rationalists at the birth of our country could not. Do we fear that atheists, agnostics, and activists of all types will be able to do in our day what no one else in history has ever been able to do? If we do, it is because we do not know "the Scriptures or the power of God." (Matthew 22:29)

The Blessed Impact Of Christ's Kingdom Upon The World's Societies

Having considered briefly the victory and expansion Messiah's kingdom in this world, let us now examine what the Holy Spirit reveals through the psalmist David about the kingdom's blessed impact upon the societies of the world.

Psalm 68 is one of the great songs about the victory of the Messiah in this world. It looks backward to the great joy and victories God gave his children as he led them through the desert. It looks forward to the death and resurrection of the Messiah with all of the benefits to mankind that follow. It rejoices in the multitudes of those who announce God's word and those who fight his battles. Those beautiful words, "Your procession has come into view, O God, the procession of my God and King into the sanctuary" (v.24) thrill us with a prophetic glimpse of his glorious triumph in this world prior to the final exaltation of the king and his kingdom. With faith in our King, we recognize his procession as it makes its way in this world to ultimate glory. "The early church…understood this psalm to foreshadow the resurrection, ascension and present rule of Christ and the final triumph of his church over the hostile world."[202]

We must avoid making the same mistake that the ancient Jews made concerning the Messiah. We need to think of Messiah's victory over his enemies, not in terms of hateful military destruction, but in terms of loving redemption and salvation. Christ told us that he came to save the world, not condemn it. In fact, "He received gifts for the rebellious, that the Lord God might dwell among them that he might set up a church in a rebellious world."[203] Jesus overcomes his enemies, not by killing them or even sending them to hell, but by loving them, redeeming them, and making them his children and enriching their lives.

In addition to depicting Jesus' victory over his enemies in this world, this psalm pictures his victory over the sorrow and suffering associated with Christ's and our perennial enemy, Satan. One of the beauties of our king is that he is as kind to us as he is crushing to those who remain his enemies despite his grace and mercy to them. Look at what is said about him,

"Sing to God, sing praise to his name, extol him who rides on the clouds—his name is the Lord—and rejoice before him. A father of the fatherless, a defender of widows, is God in his holy dwelling. God sets the lonely in families, he leads forth the prisoners with singing; but the rebellious live in a sun-scorched land." (vv. 4–6)

"You gave abundant showers, O God; you refreshed your weary inheritance. Your people settled in it and from your bounty, O God, you provided for the poor." (vv. 9–10)

"Praise be to the Lord, to God our Savior, who daily bears our burdens." (v.19)

Granted, these verses do not spell out in detail all the blessings that we enjoy in our world today, the blessed gifts that have come from the Savior. Yet they clearly reveal the loving heart of the king. God's heart is for his people's comforts and prosperity. He wills that they should be so pleased with their circumstances that they would sing praise to his name and rejoice before him. Satan brought more than creation into bondage; he brought all men into bondage with it. All his followers live in a sun-scorched land. Jesus, on the other hand, delivers men from loneliness and bondage. Settling them into rich, fertile, well-watered lands, he enables them to prosper. Furthermore, he is ever-present in their lives, bearing burdens that are too hard for them. No matter how many blessings he heaps upon us or how wonderful the times are in which we live, we still have burdens that he must sometimes lift from our hearts.

Psalm 72 is another psalm that glories in the blessings of Christ the king and extols life in his kingdom. Notice the rich blessings David mentions,

"He will judge your people in righteousness, your afflicted ones with justice. The mountains will bring prosperity to the people, the hills the fruit of righteousness. He will defend the afflicted among the people and save the children of the needy; he will crush the oppressor." (v. 2–4)

"He will be like rain falling on a mown field, like showers watering the earth. In his days the righteous will flourish, prosperity will abound till the moon is no more." (v. 6–7)

"For he will deliver the needy who cry out, the afflicted who have no one to help. He will take pity on the weak and the needy and save the needy from death. He will rescue them from oppression and violence, for precious is their blood in his sight." (vv. 12–14)

In verse 17, David promises: "All nations will be blessed through him and they will call him blessed." He reaffirms, almost word for word, what the Lord said to Abraham hundreds of years before: "...all peoples on earth will be blessed through you." (Genesis 12:3)

These verses picture oppression and violence continuing in society even as the kingdom advances. Yet they also show us God's heart for his people challenging these evils. Many of the big issues today—justice for the poor, needy, and oppressed, racial profiling, equal rights for women and the handicapped, concern for animal rights—are big issues because of God's love is resident in his people. Prior to Jesus' birth and for too long afterward they were not issues at all. The loving heart of Jesus, which historically expressed itself through the church, is finding expression today in people outside the church. Even unbelievers' minds and hearts have been sensitized by the teachings of Jesus. Most do not realize that it is because Jesus came that their hearts are now concerned with these issues. Yet there can be no other explanation for the total change in society's outlook. Once there was almost no concern for sick and dying humans. Now we have campaigns to "Save the Baby Whales," etc.

It is probably also true that few business leaders of our day recognize that our general prosperity has anything to do with the teachings of Jesus. Nevertheless, everything that promotes prosperity, i.e., education, personal health, honesty, industry, loyalty, truth, has its origins in Jesus and in the institutions provided originally by the church. Truly, prosperity has come to the people like rain falling on a mown field, like showers watering the earth. We who know Jesus and his great promises know the source of this prosperity and have abundant reason to give God the glory.

Psalms 96 through 100 are great songs of praise to God for the blessings that he gives his people throughout their lives. One of the blessings extolled is God's righteous judgment. Because Jesus spoke of the great Judgment Day, the refrain, "...he comes to judge the earth. He will judge the world in righteousness and the peoples in his truth." (Psalm 96:13) is understood by many as a reference to the judgment at the end of the world. However, it refers to his governing in this present world. The rulers in the Old Testament were called judges because a large part of their God-ordained office was to judge the people with equity. In these Scriptures, the Lord's reigning and the Lord's judging are one and the same occupation. Consequently, the joy mentioned in these several psalms comes from the equity and righteousness of the Messiah's reign, expressed through his disciples in this world. Now let us look at several of these portions and notice how they depict blessings from God to be enjoyed in this present age.

"Say among the nations, 'The Lord reigns.' The world is firmly established, it cannot be moved; he will judge the peoples with equity. Let the heavens rejoice, let the earth be glad; let the sea resound, and all that is in it; let the fields be jubilant, and everything in them. Then all the trees of the forest will sing for joy; they will sing before the Lord, for he comes, he comes to judge the earth. He will judge the world in righteousness and the peoples in his truth." (Psalm 96:10–13)

"The Lord reigns, let the earth be glad; let the distant shores rejoice...Zion hears and rejoices and the villages of Judah are glad because of your judgments, O Lord." (Psalm 97:1,8)

"Let those who love the Lord hate evil, for he guards the lives of his faithful ones and delivers them from the hand of the wicked." (Psalm 97:10)

"The Lord has made his salvation known and revealed his righteousness to the nations. He has remembered his love and his faithfulness to the house of Israel; all the ends of the earth have seen the salvation of our God. Shout for joy to the Lord all the earth, burst into jubilant song with music." (Psalm 98:2–4)

"The King is mighty, he loves justice—you have established equity; in Jacob you have done what is just and right." (Psalm 99:4)

"Shout for joy to the Lord all the earth. Worship the Lord with gladness...For the Lord is good and his love endures forever; his faithfulness continues through all generations." (Psalm 100:1,5)

I had to be very selective; otherwise, I would have quoted the whole of the psalms. The Scriptures chosen clearly teach that these blessings are experienced in this world, "through all generations." The people are rejoicing in present blessings, not blessings expected in the next world. They remember what God has done for them in the past and rejoice in what he is doing for them now. Furthermore, they are comforted by his everlasting faithfulness, knowing that he will deliver their children and their children's children from the hand of the wicked for all generations.

The overriding tone of these psalms is joy and thanksgiving, jubilation in worship. The psalmist expects that this joy and gladness will not be restricted to a little slice of land on the edge of the Mediterranean Sea, but eventually the entire earth will be so blessed as to "Shout for joy to the Lord." In the book of Deuteronomy, and many other places, the Lord promised rich blessings to his people if they would be careful to follow his directions. (See Deuteronomy 28:1–14; 30:1–10) The psalmist praises God for remembering his love and for his faithfulness in keeping his word and so enriching their lives. God has made life in the villages of the world good and glad.

The basis of all orderly society is a just ruler or a just constitution to which the society remains faithfully adhered. These psalms trace all happiness and comfort to the mighty king who loves justice and establishes equity. Henry comments, "The Christian religion as far as it is embraced, shall establish states and kingdoms, and preserve good order among men."[204]

Stott asks a question that has been asked by many who are not believers in the Lord Jesus, "Isn't it possible to expect social change unless people are converted?" Then he gives his definitive conviction. "No it isn't." He attributes, as does this book, all of the blessings we now enjoy directly to Jesus' redeeming power in the lives of men.[205]

Stott speaks of the tension between what we know to be true now and what we know will be true in the future. It is what he calls the tension between "the contemporary and the eschatological. Christians live in the present, but do so in thankfulness for the past and in anticipation of the future."[206]

Bright speaks brilliantly to this same situation in which we find ourselves today. He calls it the "tension between the victory won and the victory anything but won, between the Kingdom which is at hand and the Kingdom unseen and unrealized."[207] The great forward movement of the church described in Part I indicates that his kingdom has made great advances. The powerful pervasive presence of evil still resists every advance. We live between what life was before Christ came and what life is becoming and will be. Truly his procession is coming into view.

Are we there yet? Have all these great visions been realized? Are all our villages and cities models of holiness and goodness? Are God's directions universally loved and followed? Is God's will now being done on earth as it is in Heaven? Is justice done the world over? Has the Gospel been preached to all the world yet? Obviously, the answer to all of those questions is a resounding "No." The leaven has not yet transformed the whole lump.

Jesus told us to pray for God's kingdom to come. He would never have told us to pray for something that his heavenly Father had no intention of answering. The Father is answering that prayer every day. With every new person coming to faith in Christ, the kingdom comes a little more. Another person endeavors to do the heavenly father's will. Another person learns to love his neighbor as himself. Another voice is raised for justice. Another person administers justice in his share of the world. The king's rule and king's justice and the king's good order are extended a little farther into the societies of the world. The villages of the world are gladdened because of the increase of love, order, and harmony and their accompanying blessings. In spite of all the evil yet remaining, this world is a much better, safer, and happier place today than it has ever been, thanks to the coming of the king in his kingdom to judge the earth with righteousness and the peoples in his truth.

FOUR

God's Revelation Through The Prophets

Isaiah

After a 52-year reign in which, for the most part, King Uzziah did what was right in the eyes of the Lord, he died. (2 Chronicles 26:23) During that year, Isaiah saw the Lord, seated on a throne, high and exalted, with the train of his robe filling the temple. (Isaiah 6:1) After a half-century of relative stability, the future was very uncertain. God in his mercy and wisdom showed the youthful Isaiah a vision of a king who would never die. The king on the throne, high and lifted up, speaks of God's transcendence, his exaltation beyond the reach of his adversaries. His train, filling the temple, reveals his total involvement in the lives of those he loved and created. He revealed to Isaiah a beautiful future for mankind—the increase of God's kingdom on earth and a future assured by the eternal God.

The book of Isaiah begins with a picture of terrible spiritual and moral degradation and ends with a picture of glorious redemption and transformation. It begins with the city created by man and ends with the city transformed by God. Isaiah beautifully pictures the dramatic transformation the Messiah will bring about in history. The God David saw, sitting on his throne laughing at all opposition, Isaiah saw transforming the societies of the world for his own pleasure and glory and for their comfort and enjoyment.

This transformation and elevation of society is not the result of any sort of evolution or natural progress. It is entirely the work of the Lord of Hosts. The Holy Spirit transforms cultures by transforming men, one by one, renewing their minds according to the teachings of Jesus. Modern man, not realizing the source of all the benefits we now enjoy, sees no relationship between Jesus' kingdom and our present prosperity. Like the socialist activists of the early twentieth century, he assumes that materially changing people's environments will change their hearts and attitudes and encourage peace among men. However, "In all history there is not a shred of evidence to support that view."[208] Rather, all history testifies to the truth that wherever the Gospel of Jesus has gone, it has changed societies for the better.

Isaiah's revelation of the great redemptive work of the Lord begins in the first chapter with a picture of the terrible conditions in the city of man. The city where God chose to put his name had become a harlot. It once was full of justice and righteousness but is now full of murderers. The whole nation had become sinful, "…a people loaded with guilt, a brood of evildoers, children given to corruption! They have forsaken the Lord; they have spurned the Holy One of Israel and turned their backs on him." (1:4)

Yet, is the King on heaven's throne ready to throw in the towel and apologize to his enemies for laughing at them? Certainly not. Neither is he ready to give up on his people. In this very first chapter where Satan's influence is seen in all its ugliness, our gracious God issues one of the most compassionate invitations ever heard by men,

"Come now, let us reason together," says the Lord. "Though your sins are like scarlet, they shall be white as snow; though they are red as crimson, they shall be like wool. If you are willing and obedient, you will eat the best from the land." (1:18–19)

In addition, he promises judgment upon the unrepentant, the purification and redemption of the entire society, and the restoration of true holy leaders, so that afterward "You will be called the City of Righteousness, the Faithful City." (1:25–26)

The first chapter of Isaiah is the preface for the book. It correctly pictures the condition of men in the world and promises the great work of redemption and elevation that God will accomplish. The remainder of the book of Isaiah is the full development of everything promised in its preface.

Chapter 2 is the real start of the book. It begins with a clear picture of what the Lord intends to do in history.

"In the last days the mountain of the LORD'S temple will be established as chief among the mountains; it will be raised above the hills, and all nations will stream to it. Many peoples will come and say, 'Come, let us go up to the mountain of the LORD, to the house of the God of Jacob. He will teach us his ways, so that we may walk in his paths.' The Law will go out from Zion, the word of the LORD from Jerusalem. He will judge between the nations and will settle disputes for many peoples. They will beat their swords into plowshares and their spears into pruning hooks. Nation will not take up sword against nation, nor will they train for war anymore." (2:2–4)

Isaiah's "last days," are different from Paul's "last days" (2 Timothy 3:1). They are different times and emphasize different ideas. Isaiah's "last days," are the Gospel Age. Isaiah emphasizes what the Lord will be doing in those days. Paul's "last days," are the last days of the Gospel Age, when

Satan, convulsed with awful frustrated hostility, will attempt terrible atrocities against the victorious and blessed church.

This vision is not about heavenly experiences. The issues and events described are happenings in the realm of time. It is during our days on earth that we need to learn of God's ways so that we may walk in his paths. It is during our lifetime that we need to hear the Law of the Lord and nations need his judgments to settle their disputes. In addition, it is now that we need to make every reasonable effort to avoid going to war unless it is the only way to deal with cosmic law breakers such as Adolph Hitler and Saddam Hussein. It is during our days on earth that we need to seek honorable and just ways to settle disputes and turn our massive engineering and manufacturing capabilities into productive, not destructive, efforts.

This vision in Chapter 2 confirms Isaiah's prophecies in Chapter 9 that are the foundation of this book.

"Of the increase of his kingdom and peace there shall be no end upon the throne of David. He will reign on David's throne and over his kingdom, establishing and upholding it with justice and righteousness from that time on and forever. The zeal of the Lord Almighty will accomplish this." (Isaiah 9:7)

The Lord God showed the youthful Isaiah this beautiful picture. Its fulfillment is something to look forward to and to pray and work for. The hope of its certain coming is something to rejoice in; if not for ourselves, for our children and their children. It is indeed, "one of the great prophetic visions of all time, making articulate the immemorial longing of the human heart for peace." [209] God has revealed to us that his kingdom will usher in a day "when mankind shall live together and work together in faith and righteousness and brotherhood." [210]

I believe that it is a mistake to base all our thoughts of the future on Paul's single sentence, "In the last days, perilous times shall come." (2 Timothy 3:1) It is important to recognize that while Satan's wrath against the kingdom will increase, God's wisdom, power, and grace are more than adequate to make Jesus' kingdom triumphant and increase continually. As we look at the future, we can rely on the Bible's many plain encouraging prophetic statements relative to life on this earth as the kingdom expands its redemptive transforming influence.

The writer to the Hebrews points out that God, "In putting everything under Jesus' feet, left nothing that is not subject to him." Then he states the obvious, "…at present we do not see everything subject to him." (Hebrews 2:8) By implication he says, "Just because it hasn't happened yet, doesn't mean that it won't happen." Should we dismiss as fantasy the Lord's promise of a redeemed and transformed society, simply because it has not yet been fully realized in our midst? Should we dismiss it because it seems impossible or because it does not fit in with what we have always heard? How can we pray with faith the prayer that Jesus himself taught us if we do not believe in the possibility of a redeemed and transformed society on earth? It just does not make sense that Jesus would teach us to pray for something that God never intended to bring about. Clearly, God has been working in all of history answering that prayer. Would God allow the devil's lie to Eve to pass without completely obliterating it by demonstrating his gracious and wonderful truth? God's heavenly laughter at the anger, lies, and insults of the enemy even now reaches our ears as we experience and rejoice in all the blessings that are coming to us through the seed of our first mother. It is surely appropriate that God's love and good will toward men in placing them on this perfectly created planet should be seen by all men here on earth before everything is changed and life in the hereafter begins. God revealed to Isaiah that in the Messiah's work, "…the glory of the Lord will be revealed and all mankind together will see it. For the mouth of the Lord has spoken." (Isaiah 40:5)

Bright has beautifully expressed a wonderful truth. He believes that there is "a remarkable coincidence between the vision of the Kingdom of God as the prophets saw it and that goal which men most deeply desire today...In truth the desire of mankind is a desire for the Kingdom of God."[211] Most people in the world, in their strivings after happiness, probably do not realize or believe that, but it is the truth.

In Chapter 9, Isaiah introduces us to the ever-living King, the one who made this promise and who will eventually fulfill it. He tells us of the King's heavenly origins. He will be called, "Wonderful Counselor, Mighty God, Everlasting Father, Prince of Peace." (9:6) Then he tells us of this King's earthly origins: "A shoot will come up from the stump of Jesse: from his roots a Branch will bear fruit." (11:1) Clearly, Isaiah is speaking of Jesus the Messiah, the Son of God and the Son of David.

The remainder of Chapter 11 and Chapter 12 paint another beautiful picture of the transformation that this King who judges with righteousness will make in this world. It is truly a picture of peace and beauty and includes the wonderful promise that "...all the earth will be full of the knowledge of the Lord as the waters cover the sea." (11:9)

Isaiah nowhere discounts evil or its terrible plague upon the human race. He begins the chapter in which he introduces Jesus with a reference to the deplorable conditions that men create and must endure. Hardly any more depressing words have ever been written, nor words that more accurately describe the results of sin and rebellion against God:

"Distressed and hungry, they will roam through the land; when they are famished, they will become enraged and, looking upward, will curse their king and their God. Then they will look toward the earth and see only distress and darkness and fearful gloom and they will be thrust into utter darkness." (8:21–22)

Isaiah then counters this depressing picture with those beautiful words that have inspired us for generations, words that picture the gracious hope our redeemer King brings: "The people walking in darkness have seen a great light; on those living in the land of the shadow of death a light has dawned." (9:2) That light is Jesus and it is shining now more broadly than ever. For Isaiah and even for the disciples in the first century, it was only "the first gleam of dawn," but it is "shining ever brighter" promising the coming of "the full light of day." (Proverbs 4:18) Undeniably, much darkness still exists everywhere in the world, but the gates of hell cannot shut out the light.

These beautiful promises in Chapters eleven and twelve express the confident hope that has sustained the kingdom for over two thousand years. Nevertheless, it is more than faith and hope that has kept the kingdom advancing. It is the work of the Lord Almighty. He is behind every merciful deed, every sacrificial death, every spiritual victory, and every new believer coming into the kingdom. Because of the Cross and the Resurrection, victory is never in doubt. God's will is being done before our eyes; there is much glory yet to be seen as the kingdom advances.

In Chapter 32, God begins to reveal how his victory over sin and darkness will be achieved. He himself, through his poured-out Holy Spirit, will make it happen:

"The fortress will be abandoned, the noisy city deserted; citadel and watchtower will become a wasteland forever, the delight of donkeys, a pasture for flocks, till the Spirit is poured upon us from on high, and the desert becomes a fertile field, and the fertile field seems like a forest. Justice will dwell in the desert and righteousness live in the fertile field. The fruit of righteousness will be peace; the effect of righteousness will be quietness and confidence forever. My people will live in peaceful dwelling places, in secure homes, in undisturbed places of rest." (32:14–18)

"The zeal of the Lord Almighty," Isaiah had promised, "will accomplish this." (9:7) That promise is restated here. The kingdom of God will be introduced into this world, established and empowered by the pouring out of the Holy Spirit. As the Interpreters' Bible reminds us, "This Pentecostal outpouring of the Spirit of God was recognized by the first Christians as a sign that the new age had dawned. (Acts. 2:1–18,33) "[212] Furthermore, it is the Holy Spirit living in men that enables them to turn away from sinful selfishness and live in ways that contribute to and maintain peace and happiness.

The Holy Spirit through Isaiah reveals to us an earthly society living in a heavenly way, a society redeemed and transformed by the Holy Spirit of God. To refuse to accept this picture is to give too much credit to God's enemies and too little credit to God.

Isaiah's prophecy contains many wonderful promises and proclamations relative to the subject of this book, such as:

"Here is my servant, whom I uphold, my chosen one in whom I delight; I will put my Spirit on him and he will bring justice to the nations...In faithfulness he will bring forth justice; he will not falter nor be discouraged till he establishes justice on earth. In his law the islands will put their hope." (42:1–4)

"...I will pour water on the thirsty land, and streams on the dry ground; I will pour out my Spirit on your offspring, and my blessings on your descendants. They will spring up like grass in a meadow, like poplar trees by flowing streams. One will say, 'I belong to the LORD'; another will call himself by the name of Jacob; still another will write on his hand, 'The LORD'S' and will take the name Israel." (44:3–5)

"Declare what is to be, present it—let them take

counsel together. Who foretold this long ago, who declared it from the distant past? Was it not I, the LORD? And there is no God apart from me, a righteous God and a Savior; there is none but me. Turn to me and be saved all you ends of the earth, for I am God and there is no other." (45:21–22)

"...I am God, and there is none like me. I make known the end from the beginning, from ancient times, what is still to come. I say: My purpose will stand, and I will do all that I please...Listen to me, you stubborn-hearted, you who are far from righteousness. I am bringing my righteousness near, it is not far away; and my salvation will not be delayed. I will grant salvation to Zion, my splendor to Israel." (46:9–10,12–13)

Although these great promises are definitely written to Israel, I understand them to apply in greater measure to the true Israel, the church of Christ. They are promises of a much greater work than simply the return of Israel to the Promised Land after the exile to Babylon. Furthermore (and it is important for the purpose of this book to note this), these promises clearly relate to life on earth. The Messiah will bring justice to be enjoyed on earth. He will invite people from the ends of the earth and cause them to turn to the Lord. The worldwide spread and transforming influence of the righteous kingdom of God upon the kingdoms of earth are envisioned. All are attributed to the Lord and his Christ. These promises underscore what Isaiah wrote in 9:7. "The zeal of the Lord Almighty will accomplish this." God, Himself, claims this to be his plan. He has foretold it; he will bring it to pass. (46:10)

Isaiah 49 is truly one of the great chapters in all of Scripture. It gives abundant comfort to persons in distress and difficulty, and marvelous encouragement to the church to look forward to its ultimate triumph and glory. Much of this beautiful prophecy is actually addressed to the Messiah, assuring him of great success in his labors on behalf of the

Gentiles. The Lord tells him that just saving Israel is "too small a thing" for him and promises to make him "a light for the Gentiles," that he could take God's "salvation to the ends of the earth." (49:6) After dealing with the discouragement that God's people often feel when they look around at their circumstances, it ends with wonderful encouragement for the Lord's people. "Then all mankind will know that I, the Lord, am your Savior, your Redeemer, the Mighty One of Jacob." (49:26)

Zion's cry, echoed in verse 14, "The LORD has forsaken me, the LORD has forgotten me," is too often on the lips of the church today. I am afraid the eyes of many Christians are more on the circumstances of our generation than they are on the great prophecies and promises of the Word of God. Many fear that darkness is making progress in the world, rapidly covering the earth. They forget that that is exactly how Isaiah described conditions in the world prior to the coming of Jesus. (Isaiah 60:2) No matter how dark and threatening our times may seem to be, they are vastly lighter and brighter than they were the day Jesus was born. Furthermore, it is thrilling to know that God is at work in our time, in our world. He is fulfilling his great and gracious purposes through every one of the circumstances of our times. Scripture again and again reminds us that God reigns over all the earth. In current events "his footsteps are not known, yet he is always moving everywhere for the accomplishment of his redemptive purpose made known in Christ." [213]

In our absorption with the disheartening news televised over and over again into our homes, God calls to us, "Listen to me, my people; listen to me my nations…My righteousness draws near speedily, my salvation is on the way, and my arm will bring justice to the nations." (Isaiah 51:4) Twice he says, "Listen to me." It is as if we cannot get our minds and eyes off the things we see. He grabs us by our shoulders, looks into our faces, breaking into our discouraging reveries and disheartening conversations to make us listen to him. We must understand that his arm is at work right now, spreading his truth, justice and salvation to the nations. This is a reaffirmation of his previous pronouncement, "The zeal of the Lord Almighty will accomplish this. (Isaiah 9:7) His arm is at work. It is not idle. It is not tired. It is not crippled or ineffective. It is accomplishing his original purpose. Nothing has changed his original plans.

"We must take evil seriously...There is no naive confidence that the goodness in man will gradually triumph over the evil in him, or that Christians can bring in the Kingdom of God if they work at it hard enough."[214] Guthrie makes this astute observation, "We must not take evil more seriously than God does."[215] Do we take evil more seriously than God does? Is that why so many have such a pessimistic view of the future of life in this world? Did not Jesus rise from the dead? Did not God demonstrate his mighty power when he seated the risen Christ at his right hand in the heavenly realms, far above all rule and authority, power and dominion, and every title that can be given, not only in this present age but also in the one to come? Did not God place all things under his feet and appoint him to be head over everything for the church? (Ephesians 1:20–22) We do not know how God will bring everything to its glorious fulfillment. Nevertheless, one thing is sure: The future will glorify God, not the power of evil.

Chapter 54 speaks of the future realization of his glorious intentions:

"Enlarge the place of your tent, stretch your tent curtains wide, do not hold back, lengthen your cords, strengthen your stakes. For you will spread out to the right and to the left; your descendants will dispossess nations and settle in their desolate cities." (54:2)

The whole chapter tells of the expansion, joy, security, and righteousness of his people. It ends triumphantly:

"No weapon formed against you will prevail, and you will refute every tongue that accuses you. This is the heritage of the servants of the Lord, and this is their vindication from me, declares the Lord." (v. 17)

Chapter 60 introduces the remaining chapters in this wonderful revelation. Here the Lord reveals that the nations of the world will come to the light of the Lord. (v.3) As strange as it may seem to us today, the Lord tells us that the time will come when the kingdom will be loved and honored. (v.15) Perhaps best of all is the promise, "No longer will violence be heard in your land, nor ruin or destruction within your borders." (v.18)

In this chapter, Isaiah promised peaceful and prosperous conditions in Israel after the exile. However, its main message is for the Israel of the future, the church of Jesus the Christ. Its full accomplishment would be in the kingdom of the Messiah. Although Israel enjoyed a measure of peace and prosperity after the exile, nothing approaching the blessings promised was experienced prior to the birth of Jesus.

These last seven chapters of Isaiah contrast with the first six chapters of the book. The city man created has now become the divinely transformed city. The pictures painted in these chapters have not yet been completely realized. Nevertheless, there are many similarities to life in the United States and many other countries today. Life is truly wonderful for millions of us in the world. Never have people had it as well as they do today. We have not known poverty, hunger, discomfort, unrelieved pain, or had raging diseases that destroy millions of us. We have about 95 percent employment in good paying jobs. We have excellent educational opportunities and medical care. We enjoy peace in our neighborhoods and countries. Our churches are free to worship and serve with little restriction. They are ministering in Jesus' name very successfully all over the world. Like the first hint of dawn, Christ's light definitely shines on the horizon. Isaiah 60:1 is coming to pass: "Arise, shine, for your light has come, and the glory of the Lord rises upon you."

Ezekiel

Chapter 47 of Ezekiel is another beautiful picture of Jesus' redeeming and healing work in this world. The river spoken of here is an Old Testament equivalent of the mustard seed planted in the garden and the yeast mixed into the loaf. Since no water ever flowed out of the temple in Jerusalem, this vision is not of a literal river. This river is the kingdom of God, the church of Jesus the Christ. Proclaiming the truth that sets men free and the love that heals, this river refreshes and blesses all who are touched by it.

With a growth reminiscent of the mustard seed and the yeast, the river continually increases in width, depth, and power. It rises from ankle-deep to knee-deep to waist-deep to being so deep and wide and apparently forceful that no one can cross it. How beautifully it portrays the growth and benefit of the church/kingdom. So very small at the beginning, it could be contained in one single upper room. Soon the church filled Jerusalem with its doctrine and overflowed to Samaria. Then by the power of the Holy Spirit, it turned the world upside down, eventually capturing the emperor and the empire. The wastebasket of time is filled with the names of those who did their best to destroy it; yet the kingdom of God is more vitally alive, aggressive, evangelistic, and widespread in the world than ever before in history.

It is important to note the healing virtue of this river. Since our first parents' fall into sin, our world has been a sick society, suffering morally, mentally, emotionally, and physically. Apparently, God is not willing to take his people out of a sick world. He will vindicate his own glory and goodness by bringing relief and healing to his devastated world through the witness and ministry of his people. Note that when this powerful river, flowing out from the temple of God, empties into the sea, "the water there becomes fresh." The sea spoken of is the famous Dead Sea, a graphic symbol of the world, deadened and devastated by sin. Even in that terribly barren place, the prophet saw swarms of living creatures wherever the river flowed: "Where the river flows everything will live." (47:8–9) What an incredible promise this is concerning the influence of Christ's kingdom.

Daniel

Daniel sees a vision of a time perhaps near the end of the Gospel age. He is told, "Many will be purified, made spotless and refined, but the wicked will continue to be wicked." (12:10) This prophecy makes it clear that as long as time endures, wickedness will be present in our midst. As insistent as Scripture is that there shall be no end to the increase of God's kingdom on earth or to its blessed influences, it is just as insistent that wicked men and wickedness will never be eliminated from the earth before the Lord's return. Obviously, wicked men and wickedness have a definite presence in the societies of this world. Every new baby born has within itself the seeds of corruption and self-destruction. "As long as the world stands, there will still be in it a mixture of good and bad. Bad men will do bad things and a corrupt tree will never bring forth good fruit."[216]

Yet in spite of the hostility and efforts of wicked men and angels, there is present in the world one whose power is greater than evil. Nothing shall stop the spread and increase of Christ's kingdom or its transforming influence upon the societies of this world until the day the Lord returns.

Joel

The heart of the book of Joel is the promised outpouring of the Holy Spirit upon the Lord's people:

"I will pour out my Spirit on all people…And everyone who calls on the name of the Lord will be saved; for on Mount Zion and in Jerusalem there will be deliverance, as the Lord has said, among the survivors whom the Lord calls." (Joel 2:28,32)

This is the prophecy of Pentecost, the coming of the Holy Spirit, the great event anticipated by Jesus when he told the apostles to tarry in Jerusalem until they were endued with power from on high. Pentecost launched the Gospel age, Isaiah's "last days." Pentecost gave birth to a new race of people on earth, the true Israel. The Apostle Paul describes them as the "children of promise," whose mother is the Jerusalem that is above and free. (Galatians 4:26–28)

Immediately after the great prophecies concerning the gift of the Holy Spirit and the birth of the church, Joel gives us in Chapter 3 a picture of the Gospel age. It describes the spiritual struggle, conflict, violence, judgment, and blessing associated with God restoring the fortunes of Judah and Jerusalem. These wonderful prophecies refer to the spiritual Judah and Jerusalem, the church of the Living God that came into being on Pentecost. They certainly do not apply to the nation of Israel, which to this very day is largely still in unbelief, nor to the actual city of Jerusalem in the land of Israel. The Mount Zion and Jerusalem of which Joel speaks (2:32) out of which will come deliverance, are certainly the spiritual Zion and the heavenly Jerusalem.

Chapter 3 vividly and accurately portrays sin in the world and the conflict and victory that the church has experienced since being empowered by the promised Holy Spirit. Evil has not yielded its influence easily. It resists stubbornly to this very day. Yet God judges and promises future judgment on wickedness, while blessing and promising future blessings for his people.

Micah

"In the last days the mountain of the Lord's temple will be established as chief among the mountains. It will be raised above the hills, and peoples will stream into it." (Micah 4:1)

So begins another of the great prophecies of the increase of the kingdom of God. The last days are the Gospel days, the year of the Lord's favor (Isaiah 61:2). They appear to Micah to be glorious days. Inspired by the Holy Spirit, Micah continues revealing something of the future progress of the work of the Lord in our world.

"Many nations will come and say, 'Come let us go up to the mountain of the LORD, to the house of the God of Jacob. He will teach us his ways, so that we may walk in his paths.' The law will go out from Zion, the word of the LORD from Jerusalem. He will judge between many peoples and will settle disputes for strong nations far and wide. They will beat their swords into plowshares and their spears into pruning hooks. Nation will not take up sword against nation, nor will they train for war any more. Every man will sit under his own vine and under his own fig tree, and no one will make them afraid, for the Lord Almighty has spoken. All the nations may walk in the name of their gods; we will walk in the name of the LORD our God for ever and ever." (Micah 4:2–5)

Micah expresses confidence that although other nations are walking in the name of their gods, Israel will walk in the name of the LORD their God. Micah paints a beautiful picture of the grand scale of the ministry of Jesus in the world. There is no hint of smallness here. There is no sign of ineffectiveness. It is important to note that these prophecies are specific to life in this world, when nations will have disputes, when war can be expected. However,

Micah reveals that because of Christ's influence the nations will settle their disputes and not go to war.

This beautiful future is the result of that which is prophesied in the first verse of Chapter 4: The gospel message will go to the ends of the earth and the peoples of the world will stream into the temple. Micah's temple isn't a building in Jerusalem; it is the living temple of God, the church of Jesus. Through the transforming influence of Christ and the worldwide spread of the Gospel, the governments of the world are changed and induced to sit down and reason together and avoid the barbarity of war.

Since the prophecy of Messiah's birth in Bethlehem came true, why should we be skeptical of this prophecy given by the same messenger? It is, of course, much easier to believe prophecies that have already been fulfilled, than those as marvelous as this one yet to be realized. Christians cannot pick and choose between prophecies, believing some and discounting others. It was, after all, the zeal of the Lord Almighty that brought about the birth of the baby in Bethlehem. The same Lord Almighty will bring these other prophecies to reality.

Zechariah

To the voices of all the prophets and saints previous to him, Zechariah adds this great prophecy:

"Rejoice greatly, O Daughter of Zion. Shout, Daughter of Jerusalem! See, your king comes to you, righteous and having salvation, gentle and riding on a donkey, on a colt, the foal of a donkey...He will proclaim peace to the nations. His rule will extend from sea to sea and from the River to the ends of the earth." (Zechariah 9:9–10)

Jesus proclaimed that his kingdom was not a political kingdom in this world. If it were, he claimed, his servants would fight to prevent his being arrested by the Jews.

(John 18:36) The kingdom, therefore, that Zechariah says will increase until it extends from sea to sea and from the River to the ends of the earth is a spiritual kingdom, a kingdom of truth and righteousness. It is a kingdom made up of peacemakers, who, like their king, are gentle and offensive only to ungodliness and falsehood. Unlike the kingdoms of this world that are extended by guns and explosives, God's kingdom will be extended by the all-conquering power of love and truth. As it increases, sometimes rapidly, sometimes more slowly, it wins the minds and emotions of men, overcomes their hostilities and revengeful spirits, so making peace. First there is peace in the heart, then in the home, then in the community, and then in society at large. Peace makes for stability in society and enables men to labor without loss from war and evil aggression. Peace opens the way to intellectual progress and thus paves the way for commercial and economic progress and release from the bondages caused by ignorance and brutality.

The 14th chapter of Zechariah, in its apocalyptic language, emphasizes all that has been heretofore highlighted from Old Testament Scriptures. If one believes, as I do, these prophecies regarding Israel and Jerusalem apply to the true Israel—the church—then this chapter underscores all that has previously been noted regarding the increase and extent of the Kingdom of the Messiah.

FIVE

God's Revelation In The New Testament

The Gospel Of Matthew

Jesus, in the Sermon on the Mount, taught us to lift up to our heavenly Father the following petition: "Our Father in heaven, hallowed be your name, your kingdom come, your will be done on earth as it is in heaven." (Matthew 6:9–10)

Christians understand the kingdom of God to be the reign of Jesus in the hearts of men. It is not something that will be inaugurated after the return of the Lord Jesus in glorious splendor. It is now a powerfully present force in this world and is continually increasing its influence.

Isaiah prophesied that there would be no end to the increase of Messiah's kingdom. Jesus here teaches us to pray for that increase to be realized on earth. Jesus tells us to pray that our heavenly Father's name be hallowed and his kingdom extended and his will be done on earth as it is in heaven.

Please note that Jesus used the words, "on earth."

Would Jesus ask us to pray for something that he knows will never come to pass on earth? Does not this one request speak clearly and precisely Jesus' own heart's desire? Does not Jesus, who came to do his Father's will, want everyone on earth to hallow and love the Father and do his beautiful will? This petition may be the most important request in this beloved prayer. Should we glibly recite it without ever expecting it to be answered? Jesus would not teach us so to pray.

To say that Jesus died only to forgive us our sins and take us out of this sin-cursed world to a better place speaks too much of pessimism and of Divine weakness. Did he not die to validate his Heavenly Father's love and intention for men? Did he not die to bring to earth some of the glory of the heavenly place where everyone joyfully does the Father's will? I am sure God's heart rejoices when he sees us enjoying and earnestly sharing the great benefits that come to us through Jesus. Every blessing from God shames and ridicules the devil who promised so much and delivered nothing but pain, sorrow, and death.

Consider the following statements of Jesus relative to the increase of his kingdom:

"From the days of John the Baptist until now, the kingdom of heaven has been forcefully advancing, and forceful men lay hold of it." (Matthew 11:12)

"And I tell you that you are Peter, and on this rock I will build my church, and the gates of Hades will not overcome it." (Matthew 16:18)

Christ speaks of violent opposition to his kingdom and of forceful victorious advance in spite of the opposition. The gates of Hades will be forcefully broken down and the captives liberated. Jesus knows that the kingdom of heaven will advance and increase throughout the Gospel Age. The kingdom does not always have an easy time. Sometimes heads roll, disciples' heads, that is. Sometimes citizens of his kingdom are honored; sometimes they are burned at the stake or stoned to death. Yet the kingdom advances. Jesus will build his church throughout all ages, and the forces of Hell cannot stop it. "The site from which Voltaire hurled septic thunderbolts is later occupied by the headquarters of a Bible society. Kingdoms topple, ideologies pass away...but the church endures."[217]

Matthew ends his Gospel with Jesus commanding his followers to make disciples of all nations. It sounds to me that he expected God, working through us, to answer that important first petition of the Lord's prayer.

"All authority in heaven and on earth has been given to me. Therefore go and make disciples of all nations, baptizing them in the name of the Father and of the Son and of the Holy Spirit, and teaching them to obey everything I have commanded you. And surely I am with you always, to the very end of the age." (Matthew 28:18–20)

One need not look far in the Scriptures or listen long to Jesus to discern that God's eye is on all the peoples of the earth. His heart beats for the salvation of all nations. He intends to bring some of the glory of the eternal world to their temporal world. Jesus' vocabulary did not contain the words "doubt" and "defeat." "We need not long pause to ask how the sense of world mission came to the early church...It came from the lips and life of Christ." [218]

The authority and the ability to take the Gospel to the entire world are resident in the person of Christ. Christ has established his kingdom in this world and has what it takes to extend it to the ends of the earth. All authority in heaven and on earth has been given to him. No one can successfully oppose him. The invasion from heaven will succeed. "God has placed all things under his *(Jesus')* feet and appointed him to be head over everything for the church, which is his body, the fullness of him who fills everything in every way." (Ephesians 1:22) There shall be no end to the increase of his kingdom and peace. "The zeal of the Lord Almighty will accomplish this." (Isaiah 9:7)

The Acts Of The Apostles

It is not surprising that the first chapter of the Book of the Acts of the Apostles records that the disciples inquired about the establishment of the kingdom of Israel. It seemed a natural thing. Jesus was alive from the dead. The Jews and the Romans had not been able to defeat him, even with a crucifixion. The disciples had never heard of his ascension and did not know that it was coming. All they knew was that Jesus was with them. He had been dead. He was now alive. The question, deep and strong in their hearts, came easily to their lips, "Lord, are you at this time going to restore the kingdom to Israel?" (Acts 1:6)

His answer to their passionate question must have shocked them beyond measure. Without mentioning the kingdom, he spoke of extending it far beyond anything that they had previously comprehended. "You will receive power when the Holy Spirit comes on you; and you will be my witnesses in Jerusalem, and in all Judea and Samaria, and to the ends of the earth." (Acts. 1:8)

"To the ends of the earth"—the Lord saw the church/kingdom going victoriously over all opposition to the very ends of the earth. He did not see a weak, ineffective church. He expressed no doubt. He never suggested that the advance of his kingdom would depend upon Caesar's attitude toward it or the Jew's acceptance of this new expression of their ancient faith. Jesus simply stated, "You will be my witnesses...to the ends of the earth." (Acts 1:8)

And they were. They filled Jerusalem with their doctrine (Acts 5:29). They invaded and brought great joy to Samaria (Acts 8:8). They planted Christians in Caesar's household (Philippians 4:22). They turned the world upside down (Acts 17:6 KJV), even though people everywhere were talking against them (Act 28:22). The spread of the kingdom began on the day of Pentecost, and it continues today. Indeed, there shall be no end to the increase of his government and peace. Pentecost assured that it would be so.

A Concluding Statement On The Scriptural Teaching Of The Increase And Impact Of The Kingdom Of God

The scriptural teaching on the increase and impact of the kingdom of God is based on the nature and character of God.

The God revealed to us in the Scriptures is an awesome God; always victorious, always faithful to himself and to his people. He is a God who delights in showing mercy, not exercising judgment. He is a God who loves his people and delights in seeing them enjoy life in this wonderful world that he created. God is never discouraged or defeated by the presence or designs of his evil enemy. He will never abandon his people to his enemy. He became their Kinsman Redeemer, redeeming them from captivity to sin by the sacrifice of his own life. God will not be content with only a few people. He not only sends his servants, but goes himself to the ends of the earth with his great and gracious invitation: "Come unto me, ye who labor and are heavy laden, and I will give you rest." (Matthew 11:28)

Perhaps best of all, the Scriptures reveal a God who has taken up his residence within his people, who will always be with his people, even to the end of the age and forever. His powerful presence in their hearts enables them to shake off the effects of sin upon their lives: the attitudes that corrode personalities and curdle relationships, the habits that destroy mind and body and the practices that ruin God's great natural gifts and spiritual blessings. He fills them with a love that blesses homes and families and neighborhoods—a love that gives them goals that benefit others and glorify God—a love that expresses itself in compassion for all in need and actions appropriate to that compassion. He is a God who works his amazing wonders through his own people to raise society from the degradation that sin has brought. He teaches them to pray for his will to be done on earth as it is in heaven (Matthew 6:9–10). Jesus over and over promised to give us what we ask for in prayer. With such repeated promises, he encourages us to look forward to the day when that wonderful prayer will be answered. In so doing, God will complete the plan he had before the foundation of the world. His plan has never wavered. It has never changed. It will never fail.

Our Christ is pictured in Scripture as going forth conquering and to conquer. It pictures uncountable multitudes "…from every nation, tribe, people and language standing before his throne." (Revelation 7:9) They listen to the shouts of heaven's inhabitants "…saying: Amen! Praise and glory and wisdom and thanks and honor and power and strength be to our God forever and ever. Amen!" (Revelation 7:12)

In spite of the opposition, hatred, violent acts, and deceit of the enemy, there shall be no end to the increase of his kingdom and peace on the throne of David until in the fullness of time he will have brought "all things in heaven and on earth together under one head, even Christ." (Ephesians 1:10) Neither God nor the Scriptures speak of a Post-Christian era.

Christians believe that the Gospel of Christ will be preached to all nations. This has been a commonly understood truth since the beginning of the church. The scriptural revelation that has been neglected is that when preached to all nations the Gospel will powerfully impact all of those nations. The kingdom will not only go to all nations, it will increase powerfully in those nations, changing them for the better. God will vindicate his own person and good intentions in this world. He will fulfill the promises made to our fathers, if not for us in our lifetimes, for our children in future generations. The enemy will fume and rage and conspire and do terrible things, but he cannot stop God from redeeming men, recreating devastated societies the world over, and bringing great joy to their cities and great glory to himself.

However depressed and discouraged the ancient Jews became with all the troubles they experienced because of their unbelief and rebellion, their prophets promised the people of God a glorious future. They called Israel to be God's messengers to the world. The Old Testament Scriptures, the Bible of the early church, express a great faith in God's ability to transform both men and societies. This book calls the twenty-first century church to this same confidence; a confidence based not upon the improving circumstances of our day, but upon the character of our God and his Scriptures. Our confidence is substantially strengthened and supported by an understanding of how Christ has been changing life in our world for the better. The believer's confidence in God's faithfulness concerning the future of his kingdom is the same as that expressed by the apostle Paul to the new believers in Philippi. "He who began a good work in you will carry it on to completion until the day of Christ Jesus." (Philippians 1:6) Someone has aptly put it, "History is His story." It is a wonderful story with a happy ending, an ending already described in his Word and made certain by God's own demonstrated power over the enemy.

Sometimes the local church does not look all that alive, let alone powerful. Sometimes the preacher is boring, the congregation sleepy, the vision lacking, and its activities irrelevant. However, out of sleepy little churches sometimes arise great preachers and prophets, missionaries that go to the ends of the world with the love of Jesus. It is a mistake to judge the future of the world by what seems to go on in your local church or neighborhood. Judge the future of the world by the King of the kingdom. Look at the big picture. Look at what Christ has done in this world. Look again at what he is doing now all over this world. The gates of hell are yielding. The King is carrying forward his kingdom to a glorious victory.

"For unto us a child is born, to us a son is given,
And the government will be on his shoulders.
And he will be called Wonderful Counselor, Mighty
God, Everlasting Father, Prince of Peace.
Of the increase of his government
and peace there will be no end.
He will reign on David's throne and over his king-
dom, establishing and upholding it with justice and
righteousness from that time on and forever.
The zeal of the Lord Almighty will accom-
plish this."   *(Isaiah 9:6–7)*

"I will build my church and the gates of Hades
will not overcome it." (Matthew 16:18)

EPILOGUE

Several persons have expressed reservations about the idea that the kingdom of Jesus is continuing to improve our world, making these the best times the world has ever known. They believe the times, far from getting better, are getting worse, even perilous, which they think the Bible predicts.

Many of the problems people have with the ideas presented in this book arise out of their perceptions: perceptions of what is happening in our world today and perceptions of what life was like in the past. If one has incorrect perceptions of what life was like in the past, then his perceptions of whether life is better or worse in the present than it was in the past may not be supported by actual facts.

Having said this about perceptions, consider the objection, "The times are not getting better, but in fact they are worse than in the past." Such statements as the following indicate that many people have a more positive view of the past than is warranted. "They don't build cars like they used to. I wish I could have lived in Bible times. When we were little, no one ever locked the doors of his house. I remember when Sundays were holy days, and almost everyone went to church. You never used to hear cursing on television. We really used to learn in school. It wasn't all fun and games when I went to school."

There is, no doubt, some truth in such "reminiscences." However, they do not prove that the past was better than now. They illustrate that some people may have a more positive view of the past than is warranted. An overly positive view of the past will negatively influence one's perception of the present. If the past appears wonderful, then life in the present will have to be perceived as wonderful as well, or it will be perceived as not as good as the past. It seems that it has always been so. The past has always seemed better to some degree than the present. Nostalgia is not new. Long ago Solomon advised, "Do not say, 'Why were the old days better than these?'" (Ecclesiastes 7:10)

From the beginning of recorded time until 60 or 70 years ago, one's perceptions of the past and present arose out of two primary sources:

• The experiences and events one remembered.

• The information (perceptions) passed on by parents and grandparents, neighbors, teachers, clergy and the magazines, newspapers, and books that one read. In the 1920s radio became a source of information for many. Even then, every one of the radio newsmen had his own right or wrong perceptions that he passed along.

Today, however, we have a powerful, pervasive molder of perceptions that influences every one of us. It is television. I am persuaded that television is the major reason why the public's perception of these days is so extremely negative. I grew up in western New York State before the advent of television. There was no electricity available on the rural road where I lived. Consequently, there was no radio in my home. My parents were very poor, so there were no newspapers or magazines coming regularly into the home. The only source of information our close neighbors and we had was word of mouth, passed along by people we met who had greater access to radio, newspapers, and magazines. For instance, I did not hear of Hitler's invasion of Holland until I read about it in *The Weekly Reader* at school, several days after it had happened. A person could have axed his neighbor to death in a village 20 miles away from our home, and we might never have heard of it. Our views of life in those pre-television days were almost entirely created by our experiences. If they were good, and many of them were, then we remember life back then as wonderful.

Things are very different today. Because of wonderful technology and our more general affluence, an atrocity that takes place thousands of miles away–perhaps in Africa, England, San Francisco, or China–will be on television screens within the hour in nearly every home in America. And not just once; the average person will see the picture of the terrible act and all its gory details perhaps two dozen times over a period of several days. Each time he sees it, the erroneous perception that the times are getting more and more terrible is strengthened in his consciousness.

Occasionally a television news show will feature a *"Heartwarming"* event, perhaps as often as once a week. Yet for whatever reason, television broadcasts typically do not regularly feature news about positive events or achievements. Consequently, viewers do not receive a balanced picture of the present times.

The December 16, 1996, *U.S. News and World Report,* reported on a study of the perceptions of Americans. The results of this study confirm the power of television to mis-shape people's perceptions of their times. The study demonstrates clearly how television's continual and vivid presentation of actual events can distort one's perception of reality. In general, the study indicated that most people felt that in the United States everything was going wrong, but in their own particular community, they felt things were going very well. For instance, most people expressed their conviction that in the nation schools were failing, crime was increasing, marriages were falling apart, and health care was in serious trouble as far as quality and availability were concerned. However, in their communities, schools were good to excellent, crime was not a major problem, hospitals and doctors were excellent, and their lives were good and stable.

One very important point is that when these studies were conducted, the actual facts of the situation were much more in harmony with the participants' views of life in their communities than with their perceptions of what was going on in the nation. The actual facts, according to the report, indicated that students consistently scored better on tests than their parents did; more students finished high school; blacks and whites graduated from high school at equal rates; drug use was far below previous rates; violent crime was declining; life expectancy was growing and the black middle class was increasing rapidly. Gratifyingly, other studies by criminologists, reported by Editors Buncher and Donziger in *Crime and Punishment in the United States* and *The Real World of Crime* respectively, report the same reality and the same misperceptions. For instance, most people, because of television's constant emphasis upon crime in the news believe that street crime is increasing, yet in actual fact, it has decreased by 17 percent from its peak in the 1970s.[219]

U.S. News and World Report's summary of the study is remarkably relevant and powerfully persuasive of the argument I am now making. "Perhaps more than any single force television stokes the apocalypse now mindset by making the atypical seem more common place, even as it dims the memory of past hardships."[220] The above summary statement explains why some people, hearing the premise of this book, were skeptical and others rejected it entirely. They have been persuaded by television's constant bombardment of evil events that the good old days are gone, and that we are certainly in the perilous "last days" spoken of by the Apostle Paul.

Television has also reshaped our perceptions of the past. The continual focus on violence on television has made the past, by comparison, seem more wonderful than it really was. The violence of the past that we may have read about in school or history books or old magazines does not seem as real to us as that which we see nightly on the news shows.

This is not to deny that there were good times in the past or to imply that people today have no difficulties and troubles. Life is not perfect in the twenty-first century; it will never become perfect on earth. However, the truth is that many people's perceptions of reality have been so distorted by television that they have failed to notice how truly wonderful and easy life is becoming. Regardless of our perceptions, the facts indicate that people living in the parts of the world where the kingdom of God has been most influential have never had it as good as they do today.

Some, reading the above, may agree that life for us is physically much better than it has ever been. We are healthy and wealthy and life is physically easy. Nevertheless, they may ask about the moral conditions in our country. What about the obsession with sex and sexual freedom on television and in life? What about the tendency of people to forsake traditional marriage for 'relationships'? What about the high divorce rate? What about the restrictions being placed upon Christians today, such as their inability to have Bible reading and prayer in school? What about the emergence of the often-belligerent gay and lesbian community with their parades, picketing, and marriages? What about the tremendous pressure Pro-Choice supporters exert upon our congressional representatives and the Supreme Court? Does not all of this indicate that the kingdom of God/the church is not as effective today as it was in the past?

On the surface, the answer to the above question might

seem to be, "Yes." However, I do not believe that answer is correct. It is true that the powerful moral voice of the church was severely muted by the influence of liberal theology during the late nineteenth century and for a good portion of the first half of the twentieth century. Out of this vacuum arose the sexual revolution of the sixties, which threw off many of the cultural restraints of the Judeo-Christian heritage of our nation. Did we then suddenly become un-Christian after being Christian for so long? No, these changes simply reveal that because of the muted moral voice of the church for the first fifty years of the twentieth century many persons' actions were controlled more by lingering cultural standards than by spiritual convictions. Now as we begin the twenty-first century, there is much evidence that the church has regained its moral voice and is making a powerful impact upon society. Chapter 4 in Part I dramatically illustrates this truth.

Again, some see the often hostile and successful legal actions taken against traditional Christian practices of school prayer, invocations at public functions, and displaying the Ten Commandments in public buildings as indications of the church's failure. I disagree completely. "We are missing the point terribly if we do not see that a faith which is as definite as the Gospel of Christ is now and always will be a stone of stumbling and an occasion of offence."[221] The more aggressive and positive the kingdom of God becomes, the more offence it is going to give and the more hostility it is going to create against itself.

Richard Collier,[222] the biographer of William Booth, the founder of the Salvation Army, reports that soon after it was founded savage attacks were levied against its members. Over 600 officers in the Salvation Army were brutally assaulted in one year. The opposition to the ministry of the Salvation Army was so intense that even an infant dedication service expressed total commitment to Jesus. Parents confessed to the Lord and to the Salvation Army their recognition and their willingness, should God permit it, that their children be "despised, hated, cursed, beaten, kicked, imprisoned, or killed for Christ's sake."[223] This information illustrates my belief that the present attacks on Christian traditions and values are reactions against a church that is coming alive and threatening the ease of those whose viewpoints and values are opposite ours. Such strong reactions may indicate that persons, who were not seriously offended by the cultural Christianity of the late nineteenth and the early twentieth century, are now feeling the heat of genuine Christianity and are rising up to counterattack. It may be impossible to prove that evil's aggression is its response to a reawakened church, but I think there are indications that it is so.

The Apostle Paul in Chapter 6 of Ephesians pictures this world system as a mighty confederation of evil.[224] We should not be surprised that the world system hates Christ. "We cannot be rightly prepared for the fierce struggle of our generation if we do not understand the intensity of the opposition to a committed Christianity."[225] Jesus revealed to John about God's enemy and ours, "He is filled with fury, because he knows his time is short." (Revelation 12:12) The intense opposition expressed against traditional Christian values and moral absolutes in our country today indicates the strength of the church, not its failure. It is a good omen, because it speaks of a more vigorous assault upon the gates of hell than has previously been waged. The church should be encouraged when its witness and effort disturb evil enough to cause it to rise up, using every means at its disposal to try to overcome us. Like the first followers of Jesus, we can rejoice if we are called to suffer for Jesus' name. (Acts 5:41)

This opposition to Christ in our society bodes well for the Christian faith and for the future of the nation. History has clearly demonstrated that the church is the healthiest and most effective when it has opposition. Acts 28:22 tells us that people everywhere were speaking against the Christians, yet they had tremendous success. The kingdom of God did not need popular approval or support to succeed. The church was born in the fire and prospered in the fire for well over two hundred years. Only when it became fully legal under Constantine did it begin to gradually lose its cutting edge. The record of the church indicates that the "flourishing of Christian faith and the effectiveness of Christian witness is not contingent upon, and indeed may be blunted by, a hospitable legal and social environment." [226] Furthermore, it is probably correct to say that the unofficial and casual acceptance of the Judeo-Christian traditions at all levels of government for well over 150 years actually made most American Christians casual and lackadaisical about their faith and about propagating it.

History has also clearly demonstrated that the church, when it truly was the church, richly blessed the nation in which it dwelt, even if a majority did not embrace the Christian faith personally. Scripture has indicated that God's righteous kingdom is going to continually increase, whether the world system likes it or not. We should be encouraged about the future.

It is encouraging to believe that a bright future for both the church and the nation does not require that the United States must become officially a Christian nation or even that committed Christians must become a numerical majority. It does require those who call themselves Christians to be true, biblical Christians. It involves them living their lives in harmony with the moral absolutes of Scripture, not with what is "culturally" acceptable. Whatever the circumstances of their lives, whether in peace or in war, in poverty or in plenty, in favor or out of favor, in the majority or in the minority, it demands that Christians reflect the love that Jesus demonstrated in all of their relationships: personal, professional, and political.

How do Christians live out their faith and reflect Jesus

love? They enter the struggle for justice as Martin Luther King and William Wilberforce did, whether it be in their neighborhoods or on the national scene. They minister to the needy as the early Christians in the Roman Empire did and as World Vision volunteers do today. They visit and minister to the imprisoned as thousands upon thousands of Prison Fellowship volunteers do. They witness to the unsaved and unreached peoples of their neighborhood and the world as the believers did in the first century and as Campus Crusade and InterVarsity and Wycliffe and Trans World Radio volunteers do today. The bright future simply requires that the church be the church that the Lord intends it to be and as it now appears to be becoming again.

It is true that "Blessed is the nation whose God is the Lord." (Psalm 33:2) Yet it is a serious mistake to look to the government to bring our country into line with the revealed absolutes of the Bible. Colson is correct in his judgment that the "Jews of first-century Palestine missed Christ's message because they, like many today, were conditioned to look for salvation in political solutions."[227] It is right for a moral majority or minority to make its wishes known at the ballot box. It is wonderful and right when Christians win elections to public office and let their Christian convictions influence the bills they write and for which they vote. Yet we must not try to establish the Kingdom of God by government action.

It does not appear from Scripture that Jesus ever intended to establish a political kingdom on earth. In fact, Jesus said exactly the opposite, "My kingdom is not of this world," he told the Roman governor. (John 18:36) We should remember his words, lest we make our focus as Christians to be political rather than evangelical. It may be tempting to try to control the morality and culture of our country by laws and court decisions as Colson claims the so-called "Christian New Right" is trying to do.[228] We Christians need to remember that as beneficial as Jesus' wonderful instructions for life are, Jesus had no expectation that unbelievers and persons who hated him would make any attempt to obey them. Neither does it appear that Jesus expected Christians to force others to obey his words. Whenever Christians have seriously tried this, as in the Massachusetts Bay Colony,[229] it has always proved to be disastrous and harmful to the Christian witness itself. Christ's precepts, as inner and intense as they are, are hard enough for Christians to truly keep. We are fairly good at loving those who love us, but not as good at loving those who disagree or even despise us. How can we expect unsaved and unregenerate men to accomplish what even Spirit-indwelt believers often have difficulty doing?

Some, fearing the world, have withdrawn from the world. This has always been a mistake, an expression of doubt rather than faith. "Nowhere in the New Testament does God direct his children to found a special nation and locate in a certain geographical place, not even in the old Promised Land of Canaan." [230] Whenever Christians withdrew from the world and formed small settlements for "Christians only," they atrophied. None of these experiments has ever been strikingly successful in maintaining and governing itself for any considerable period of time. Nor has any such movement ever significantly positively influenced the secular society of its day or reached out to make disciples of anyone.

Jesus expected that the church should live in the world, yet not be of it. He expected the church not to retreat but to make disciples in all nations. History has demonstrated that, enabled by the indwelling Holy Spirit, the church/kingdom can face the most belligerent opposition and conquer by love. These are exciting days for the children of God.

Before I end this epilogue, I want to discuss briefly an anticipated objection to the idea that the physical, almost miraculous, blessings we enjoy today are ours because of Jesus. I am speaking of such blessings as modern medicine,

modern communications, modern travel, and the luxurious living that almost all in the Western world enjoy. Some, I am sure, will argue that we enjoy these blessings today, not because Jesus and his church lifted us out of the Dark Ages, but because the rationalists of the Renaissance and the Age of Reason threw off the intellectual constraints of the medieval church and introduced us to the blessings of science. I anticipate this objection because until I began this study, this was my understanding of history. Obviously, I had come to this conclusion in high school and never questioned its veracity. Probably this is also true of many people. "Wherever we locate the transition to the modern world, we are still inclined to assume that it had its origins in the Renaissance."[231] But that perception, even if it was gained in the classroom, is a wrong one.

Since I have shown in Chapter 3 that Christian Reformers introduced us to the world of science, I do not need to retrace that path. I will simply point out that "the Renaissance centered in autonomous man, while the Reformation centered in the infinite-personal God who had spoken in the Bible." [232] We learn from Scripture that man is a morally fallen being. History has undeniably demonstrated the truth of Scripture in this regard. During the thousands of years prior to Christ, un-enlightened by divine revelation, enslaved by ignorance and passionate brutality, sinful man brought few significant scientific achievements into existence. He was able to construct magnificent palaces and pyramids, but at the cost of the lives of thousands of slaves who were driven to their deaths by the extreme labor. He could melt and mix metals and make plows and swords, but he could not make peace. He could sail around the edges of the continents by observing the stars, but he could not lift himself a foot off the ground. He could boast of the invention of a wheel, but nothing to move it except pure brute strength, his own or some beast's.

Jesus, the Son of God, did not indicate that we could discover truth by looking into ourselves. On the contrary, he claimed to be truth incarnate. (See John 14:6) He taught that the way to discover the truth that liberates is to listen to his words. (see John 8:31–32) We will not argue that the thinkers and writers of the Renaissance period made no contribution whatsoever to the advance of civilization. We will argue only that the humanistic rationalist's return to the study of the ancient pre-Christian classics, which were man-centered and often morally corrupt, brought no new light into the world. The Christian reformers, convinced that God is the essence of truth and that his creation is as certain a divine revelation as is the Bible, were impelled to relentlessly study and seek God in his created universe as diligently as they sought him in the Bible. This drive to search out the truth and to follow wherever it might lead is exactly the scientific method. Consequently, it was they who introduced us to it and to all the discoveries that have ushered in the modern world.

It was not the backward-looking, inward-looking humanistic rationalists who gave us the wonderful blessings we now enjoy. They are the gifts of the children of the kingdom of God, the upward-looking Christian thinkers, willing to lay down their lives if necessary to follow Jesus, who said, "I am the Truth." (John 14:6) Their search after God was a search for truth; their search for truth was a search for God. We are the blessed beneficiaries of their honest, diligent, prayerful searching and wonderful discoveries.

"If you hold to my teaching, you are really my disciples.
Then you will know the truth, and
the truth will set you free."
(John 8:31–32)

Appendix

The transformation that the kingdom of God has brought to this world has it foundation in truth. It will be helpful, I think, to consider the convictions that have motivated and guided Christians to minister so zealously in the name of Jesus.

The Convictions That Guided Christians In Their Ministries

The expressions of love that we discussed in Chapters Three and Four of Part I are not different in nature from all other efforts to reform society. All are motivated by and express Jesus' love for mankind. For instance, the person who would minister to the sick would likely support efforts to free the slave, educate the illiterate, improve conditions in prisons, and elevate the condition of women. Therefore, as we consider the convictions that guided Christians throughout history, we will not confine ourselves to health issues.

One of the most basic convictions of Christians involved in the effort to relieve the pain of mankind is that sin is the central problem of society. "I" is the center letter in the word sin. The sinful self, dedicated to gratifying itself whatever the cost, is behind the political and social chaos on this beautiful planet.

The Rev. Walter Rauschenbusch (1861–1918), while serving as pastor of an immigrant congregation in New York City, became painfully aware of the suffering of the members of his congregation and their companions in the poverty-stricken neighborhoods of his parish. The exploitation of the poor by the leaders of industry and the indifference of those in seats of power in the city greatly distressed him. It did not seem either sufficient or biblical to him that all the church had to offer to suffering humanity was a home in heaven. He began an intense study of the Scriptures to discover what the Bible had to say about the attitudes his people should have concerning the problems they were facing. As a result of his extensive study of Scripture and his experience in the pastorate, Rauschenbusch correctly diagnosed for all of us Christians the nature of the problems impacting our world and clearly identified the solution. He brought to the church's attention the centrality of sin in producing the social problems that injure so many. He also saw that the coming of the kingdom of God was the answer.[233]

Rauschenbush was correct in identifying sin as the culprit behind the conflict that has plagued the human race. This is true. It may be a struggle between a husband and wife in the home that ends in stagnation, divorce, or murder. It may be the struggle between nations that leaves countless dead and maimed on the battlefield, communities and countryside devastated, homes in ashes and refugees by the millions. Whatever the conflict, the culprit behind it is sin. Sin is the only real explanation for the total callousness of the ancient world toward the poor, ailing, enslaved, and the victims of war. Sin explains why racism, greed, immorality, and poverty linger into the modern world. Sin is the reason the story of the human race is such a tragic bloody tale.

Jesus is certainly the Savior of the world. The angel said to Joseph, in announcing Jesus' birth, "You are to give him the name Jesus, because he will save his people from their sins." (Matthew 1:21) Too long we have seen this only as a reference to individuals being saved from their sins and having their eternal destiny changed from hell to heaven. We can thank Rauschenbush for pointing out to us the immediate impact that delivering individual men from their sins, thus increasing the sway of the kingdom of God, will have on their own lives and on the experience of all mankind. Jesus taught us to pray, "Your kingdom come, your will be done on earth as it is in heaven." (Matthew 6:10) We have prayed that prayer for two thousand years, but have not always realized what benefits would be ours if it were actually answered. More tragic is the real possibility that we never believed that Jesus intended it to be answered in the present age.

John Stott, the British theologian and philosopher, is one fully persuaded of the truth of Rauschenbush's conclusion that sin is the big problem of the human race. He asks the question, "Isn't it possible to expect social change unless people are converted?"[234] By being converted, I assume he means, being delivered from both the guilt and controlling power of sin and indwelt by the Holy Spirit through faith in Jesus. His own answer to the question is clear and definite: "No. It isn't."[235] Then he correctly claims that Jesus, through his "delivered from sin" people, has made an enormous contribution to the amelioration of all of society, not just the Christian community.

Many so-called social scientists do not believe that it is necessary for men to be delivered from their sins for civilization to be lifted from its degradation. In fact, many disagree fervently, even to the point of ridiculing the idea of man's sinfulness. Consequently, denying that sin is in the hearts of man, denying men are sinners by nature, they have tried scheme after scheme to improve men's lives. None of these schemes, based on the idea of innate human goodness, has had much success.

Perhaps the most notable of these failed schemes was socialism. With a view of human nature entirely different from the Christian viewpoint, its responses to civilization's problems and those of the industrial age in particular have been decidedly different and mostly ineffective. Socialism has had little success for the simple reason that it rejects the biblical concept of sin. The early socialists, idealistically believing in the goodness of man, were convinced that they could solve men's problems by improving their environment. Consequently and unfortunately, most of their helpful intentions were short-circuited by the meanness and selfishness of sin in men's hearts.

Other socialists, such as Marx and Engels, had no patience with this goody-goody helpful brand of socialism. They believed that the only way to redeem society was to destroy capitalism by revolution and let a new society emerge from its ashes.[236] Marx and Engels did not reckon on the presence and power of sin. What emerged from their destructive efforts was not the just society they had predicted, but something even more terrible than that which they had destroyed.

It was with this un-Christian philosophy that the communists came to power in Europe and Asia. During the last century, large portions of our world have experienced the tragedy that those ideas have inflicted on civilization. Hundreds of thousands, yes, even millions, have been impoverished, enslaved, or killed. This ideology, instead of elevating society, has reduced it to the lowest common denominator.

In the non-communist world, other idealistic non-Christian schemes for elevating society have had little success. For instance, the idea that all people needed for peace and happiness is good housing produced, instead of ideal and happy communities, the infamous "projects." Millions of dollars are being spent by the government on clinics and other programs to free men and women and youth from addiction to drugs and alcohol. It is common knowledge that almost without exception, none, except Christian faith-based programs, has been able to achieve a significant percentage of "cures." In fact, no government or economic system that has overlooked the sinfulness of man has had any significant success in liberating men from their troubles and social disorder.

The impact that Jesus and his delivered people has made upon the world for good is explained partially, at least, by the fact that neither Jesus nor his people overlooked the basic problem in the world, sin. They have not tried to change the world without first changing the men in the world. Some in the government of the United States of America are now beginning to recognize that faith-based programs are much more effective in delivering individuals from social ills and much less expensive than non-faith-based programs. The success of the Christian social movement occurs because they insist that for there to be a change in behavior there must first be a change in the heart.

When men recognize that their problems are spiritual and turn to Christ for deliverance from sin and receive the Holy Spirit as the source of a new moral energy, their lives are transformed. Clouse et.al. refer to the Christian social work that brings about this successful transformation as "reality based efforts."[237] The kingdom of God transforms the world by transforming men in the world.

Another conviction that has guided the church is that the love Christians have received from God through Jesus not only enables them to love their neighbors as themselves (Matthew 22:39) but demands that they do. John, the beloved disciple wrote:

"This is how we know what love is: Jesus laid down his life for us. And we ought to lay down our lives for our brothers. If anyone has material possessions and sees his brother in need but has no pity on him, how can the love of God be in him? Dear children, let us not love with words or tongue but with actions and in truth." (1 John 3:16–18)

The church, when it has taken these words to heart, has truly been the church that Christ intended. With great effort, sacrifice, and faithfulness the church has literally been the healing Christ in the world. The list of Christian persons involved in ministering to the world's hurts and needs is endless. Most such persons are unknown because their ministry has been done inauspiciously, without fanfare or public notice.

The love that generated intense personal and private ministry also inspired many public efforts. Every great evangelistic movement in modern history has been accompanied by significant social ministries. Wesley's ministries to the illiterate and poor of England have already been mentioned. From the evangelistic ministry of Dwight L. Moody to those of the present day, have come strong efforts to minister to the physical needs of the downtrodden and destitute. The Salvation Army, rescue missions with many different focuses, World Vision, Prison Fellowship, Habitat for Humanity, and Samaritan's Purse are recent examples. There have been many others. Clouse goes so far as to say that "The biblical teaching of love as practical assistance to those in need characterized the (church's) philanthropic reaction to industrialization."[238]

This same conviction has guided the church from the beginning. In whatever the situation Christians found themselves, whatever difficulty cursed the day in which they lived–slavery, poverty, war, despotism, or plague–the church responded by reaching out to relieve the suffering, whoever they might be, friend or foe.

The widespread missionary movement of the last two hundred years is another example of Christians obedient to the Biblical injunction to love one another. In addition to reaching souls for Christ, Christian missionaries have brought practical relief to peoples in need around the world. Although the great majority of missionaries see their primary task as winning the lost to Christ, the mission movement, nevertheless, has had an enormous impact on the quality of life in the non-western world. The introduction of modern medicine, public health, and sanitation is one very real benefit. Wherever missionaries have gone, they have built and equipped hospitals and clinics and orphanages, immunized children and adults, taught effective methods of farming, drilled wells, distributed food and clothing and done whatever was most necessary to relieve physical suffering. Today, missionaries are in the forefront of the effort to both stop the spread of HIV/AIDS and care for those orphaned by this modern plague. One of their earliest and most significant and extensive enterprises has been in the field of education and literacy development. This has had a profound impact and been a great benefit. Many, if not most, of the leaders of Third World countries over the past hundred years were trained in mission schools and universities.

Another significant conviction, perhaps more often assumed than pronounced, that has guided Christians is that Jesus did indeed intend to make life better for the people of the world. "As British historian Brian Stanley observes, most Protestant missionaries in the nineteenth century, especially those from Great Britain, believed that missions would transform heathen barbarianism into Christian civilization."[239] There is abundant reason for this often unspoken assumption.

The first is that the societies in the countries which sent the most missionaries had themselves been lifted by the Gospel from the appalling conditions of the world into which Jesus had been born. They believed the Christian influence would deliver peoples in the heathen lands from the violent and ignorant expressions of unbridled sinfulness that oppressed them.

The second is that wherever the Gospel of Jesus has gone, barbarian societies have been powerfully, positively impacted and in many instances entirely transformed by the Gospel. Christians believed that their message was indeed the message of the Savior and that it was meant to deliver and liberate men from all kinds of evil. They were confident in their message and faithful in proclaiming it, demonstrating its truth by their incredible labors. Two such Englishmen were William Wilberforce and William Pitt.

A renowned Member of Parliament in England when he became a believing Christian, Wilberforce considered leaving public life to enter the ministry. Prime Minister William Pitt persuaded him that "an active involvement in public affairs was part of one's Christian duty."[240] Thus persuaded, he stayed in politics but not for personal gain or glory. In 1786, he declared his resolve "to live to God's glory and his fellow creatures' good."[241] That he was convinced of Jesus' intention to improve conditions in this world for all men is indicated by the statement he made in 1787: "God Almighty has set before me two great objects—the abolition of the slave trade and the reformation of manners."[242] Thank God, he was so convinced. At least as far as the slave trade is concerned, he was ultimately successful. It took thirty years of faithful work and prayer, but in 1807 Parliament passed the bill that abolished the slave trade by British citizens[243].

The truth this book is proclaiming is that Jesus has vastly elevated society and brought about the wonderful living conditions we enjoy in our day. This is not to say that the improvement of the quality of life in this world was the whole intention or even the main intention of Jesus. Obviously, Scripture teaches that God's total intention for man goes far beyond this world, even beyond time, itself. Nevertheless, the amelioration of society on this temporary dwelling place is within God's intention. It is the (super)natural result of men being delivered from the destructive power of sin and regenerated by the Holy Spirit. Men filled with God's Spirit have done even greater works than Jesus, just as he promised. (John 14:12) Furthermore, the transformation of society brings glory to God and demonstrates the falsehood of Satan's words to our first mother about God's evil intentions.

Unfortunately, late in the nineteenth and early in the

twentieth century the wonderful combination of evangelical fervor and social ministry that characterized Rauschenbush became divorced. Not all of his disciples followed in his footsteps. Unfortunately, in their zeal to minister to the very visible physical and social needs of their neighbors, some lost sight of the invisible cause of society's ills. They overlooked the basic problem, sin, abandoned the Gospel message, and emphasized only the social ministry. Very unfortunately, perhaps as a reaction to this purely social emphasis, many evangelicals and those who call themselves fundamentalist Christians turned away from social ministry in favor of evangelism. It became embarrassingly common to hear sermons railing against the "Social-Gospelers." This was indeed a tragic happening—tragic for both groups and for society as well. Those who emphasized the social needs overlooked the main problem of society, sin. Not recognizing sin, they saw no need for the saving and healing grace of Jesus. Thus they became largely ineffective in most of their efforts. Those who put all their emphasis upon "saving souls" missed a great opportunity to effectively minister to the society around them. This neglect effectively handed the responsibility over to the government with mixed results at best.

The Reverend Martin Luther King, however, demonstrated during his all too brief life the conviction that Jesus' love demanded that we not only preach the Gospel of Jesus, but reach out to relieve suffering and deliver those in bondage. Unfortunately, he discovered that for many in the church the love ethic of Jesus had been corrupted to relate to what Ghandi called, "mere interaction between individuals."[244] The focus of love shifted from reaching out to the suffering to improving relationships with one's friends in the church. While people suffered all around them, the pursuit of personal holiness became the main goal of many Christians and Christian ministers. Dr. King brought many American

Christians back to the fact that personal holiness demands a determined interest in the needs of those around us. His famous speech, "I Have a Dream," thrills Christians everywhere with his vision of a human society where Christ's love has brought about a "beloved community...in which...the historic definition of justice applied to everyone."[245]

Dr. King's confidence echoes the conviction that Jesus did intend to make life better for the people of the world. Jesus did not intend that we pray for God's will to be done on earth as it is in heaven, without expecting it to happen. When Dr. King prayed that prayer, he not only expected it to be answered, but lovingly and patiently worked and longingly looked for its answer to come. He believed it would gradually become a reality through love. Dr. King believed that the love of God was strong enough to "penetrate and reform the structures of society itself."[246] Dr. King, a child of the church, demonstrated to the church and to the world that the church should be expressing its love by working for the creation of such a society. The church, in this case, the Black church, was behind the great improvement in race relations that we now rejoice in and enjoy in this country. Dr. King was not the first person, nor will he be the last, to die for the conviction that the church should express Jesus' love by creative action. Thank God that conviction is still moving the church to attack the gates of hell, and those gates are yielding. The "dream" is coming true, for which Christians praise God with joyful hearts.

BIBLIOGRAPHY

After Jesus, The Reader's Digest Association, Inc., Pleasantville, NY, 1992

Alexander, Pat, The Lion Encyclopedia of the Bible, The Reader's Digest Association, Inc., with permission of Lion Publishing Corporation, Batavia, IL, 1987

Archibald, Zogis, Discovering the World of the Ancient Greeks, Quarto Publishing Co., New York, 1991

Barclay, William, The Letters to the Galatians and Ephesians, The Westminster Press, Philadelphia, 1958

Beker, J. Christiaan, The Church Faces the World, The Westminster Press, Philadelphia, 1960

Beyond, Dawn Kruger, Ed., Publication of Wycliffe Bible Translators and JAARS, Orlando, FL 32862

Boorstin, Daniel J., Hidden History, Harper & Row, Publishers, New York, 1987

Bouwsma, William J., The Waning of the Renaissance 1550– 1640, Yale University Press, New Haven, 2000

Bright, John, The Kingdom of God, Abingdon Press, Nashville, 1953

Bruce, F.F. The Spreading Flame, M. B. Eerdmans Publishing Co., Grand Rapids, MI, 1958, 1992

Buncher, Judith F. Ed., Crime and Punishment in America, Facts on File, New York, 1978

Campolo, Tony, The Kingdom of God is a Party, Word Publishing, Dallas, TX, 1990

Campus Crusade For Christ, Inc. 2001 Annual Report, Print Service, 100 Lake Heart Drive, Orlando, FL 32832, 2001

Campus Crusade for Christ, Inc., Web site, www.ccci.org.

Casa Grande Dispatch, Donovan M. Kramer, Editor and Publisher, 200 W. Second Street, Casa Grande, AZ 85222

Chidester, David, Christianity, A Global History, Harper, San Francisco, 2000

Clouse, Robert G., Pierard Richard V., Yamauchi, Edwin M. Two Kingdoms, Moody Press, Chicago, 1993

Colson, Charles, Kingdoms in Conflict, William Morrow/ Zondervan Publishing House, Grand Rapids, MI, 1987

Colson, Charles, The Body, Word Publishing Co. Dallas, TX, 1992

Cooke, Alistair, Alistair Cooke's America, Alfred A. Knopf, New York, 1973

Cotham, Perry C, Politics, Americanism, and Christianity, Baker Book House Company, Grand Rapids, MI, 1976

Council for Christian Colleges and Universities Web site, www.CCCU.org

Cox, Harvey, Fire from Heaven, Addison-Wesley Publishing Co., Reading, MA, 1995

Daly, L. J., The Medieval University, Sheed and Ward, Inc., New York, 1961.

Dodd, C. H., The Parables of the Kingdom, Charles Scribner's Sons, New York, 1961

Donziger, Steven R., Ed., The Real World on Crime, Harper Perennial, New York, 1996

Douglass, Steve, Ministry Highlights From Steve Douglas, Campus Crusade for Christ, Orlando, FL 32832, 2004

Douglass, Steve, Fund Raising Letter, Campus Crusade for Christ, Orlando, FL 32832, November 2004.

Dowley, Tim, Ed., *The History of Christianity*, Lion Publishing, Oxford, 1977

Edersheim, Alfred, *The Life and Times of Jesus The Messiah*, Vol. I, Longmans, Green, and Co., New York, London and Bombay, 1906

FamilyLife Web site. *familylife.com/about/who_we_are.asp*

Focus on the Family Web site: *family.org*

Forman, Charles W., Ed., *Christianity in the Non-Western World*, Prentice-Hall, Englewood Cliffs, NJ, 1967

Galvin, Alice, Ed., *American Catholic Higher Education*, University of Notre Dame Press, Notre Dame, IN, 1992

Gehman, Henry Snyder, Ed., *The New Westminster Dictionary of the Bible*, The Westminster Press, Philadelphia, 1970

Grant, Michael, *The History of Ancient Israel*, Charles Scribner's Sons, New York, 1984

Griffith, G. W., *The Divine Program*, W.B. Rose, Publisher, Chicago, 1923

Gross, Richard E., *Heritage of American Education*, Allyn and Bacon, Inc., Boston, 1962

Guthrie, Shirley C. Jr., *Christian Doctrine, The Covenant Life Curriculum*, CLC Press, Richmond, VA, 1968

Hamilton, Edith, *The Greek Way*, W. W. Norton And Company Inc., New York, 1930

Hamilton, Edith, *The Roman Way*, W. W. Norton And Company Inc., New York, 1932

Harrison, R. K., *Old Testament Times*, William B. Eerdmans Publishing Company, Grand Rapids, MI, 1970

Haas, Harry, *Christianity in the Asian Revolution*, Helicon Press, Inc., Baltimore, MD, 1966

Heaton, E.W., *Everyday Life in Old Testament Times, A Charles Scribner's Sons Book*, Macmillan Publishing Company, New York, 1956

Hebrew and Greek Words of the Original, with references to the English Words, Riverside Book and Bible House, Iowa Falls, IA, 50126

Henry, Matthew, *COMMENTARY on the Whole Bible*, Zondervan Publishing House, Leslie F. Church, Ed., Grand Rapids, MI 1961

Home Schooling Web site, www.findarticles.com/cf_dis/g

Hymns of the Living Faith, Light and Life Press, Winona Lake, IN, 1951

In Focus, monthly news letter published by Wycliffe Bible Translators, P.O. Box 628200, Orlando, FL 32862–8200

Intercessor, bimonthly prayer letter published by Wycliffe USA Prayer Ministries Dept. P.O. Box 628200, Orlando, FL 32862–8200

InterVarsity Christian Fellowship Inc. Web site, www.intervarsity.org

Jamieson, Robert, Faussett, A. R., Brown, David, *Commentary, Critical and Explanatory on the Whole Bible*, Zondervan Publishing House, Grand Rapids, MI

Johnson, Paul, *A History of Christianity*, Atheneum, New York, 1976

Jungle Aviation and Radio Service Web site, www.jaars.org

Louden, Irvine, Ed., *Western Medicine*, Oxford University Press, 1997

Lyons, Albert, and Petrucelli, R. Joseph II, *MEDICINE, An Illustrated History*, Abradale Press, Harry N. Abrams, Inc., New York, 1978

Mazzolan, Lidia, Storoni, Empire Without End, Harcourt Brace Jovanovich, Inc., New York and London, 1976

Meeks, Wayne A, The Origins of Christian Morality, Yale University Press, New Haven, 1993

Meyer, Adolphe E., An Educational History of the American People, McGraw-Hill Book company, Inc., New York, 1957

Murray, Iain H., The Puritan Hope, The Banner of Truth Trust, London, 1971

Miller, Madeleine S. and J. Lane Miller, Harper's Encyclopedia of Bible Life, (Completely revised edition of the original work by Boyce M. Bennett Jr. and David H. Scott), Harper and Row, Publishers, San Francisco, 1978

Modern Reformation, Alliance of Confessing Evangelicals, 1716 Spruce St., Philadelphia, 19103

30 Days Muslim Prayer Focus, Tenth Anniversary Edition, 2001. Christian and Books, Colorado Springs, CO 80936

Pelikan, Jaroslav, Jesus through the centuries, Yale University Press, New Haven and London, 1985

Petranek, Stephen L. Editor in Chief, Discover, VOL.23, NO 12. Buena Vista Magazines, subsidiary of Disney Publishing Worldwide, 114 Fifth Ave, New York, 10011–5690

Porter, Roy, The Greatest Benefit to Mankind, W. W. Norton & Company, New York, London, 1997

Prayerline, JAARS, Waxhaw, NC 28173

Prison Fellowship International Web site, www.pfi.org/international.htm

Promise Keepers Web Site, www.promisekeepers.org

Rawcliffe, Carole, Medicine and Society in Later Medieval

England, Alan Sutton Publishing Limited, Phoenix Mill (England) 1995

Roberts Today, Roberts Wesleyan College and Northeastern Seminary, Rochester, NY 14624 Summer 2004

Schaeffer, Francis A., How Should We Then Live? Fleming H. Revell Company, Old Tappan, NJ, 1976

Sheets, Tara E., Ed., Encyclopedia of Associations, Gale Group, 27500 Drake Rd., Farmington Hills, MI 48331, 1999

Sine, Tom, WILD HOPE, Word Publishing, Dallas, TX 1991

Stanley, Brian, The Bible and the Flag, Apollos, Leicester, England, 1990

Stott, John, The Contemporary Christian, Intervarsity Press, Downers Grove, IL 60515, 1992

Today, Dec. 2004, Campus Crusade for Christ, 100 Lake Drive,4200, Orlando, FL 32832

The Interpreter's Bible, Abingdon Press, New York, 1953

The NIV Study Bible, Kenneth Barker, Ed., Zondervan Publishing House, Grand Rapids, MI 49530, 1995

The Pilgrim Hymnal, The Pilgrim Press, Boston and Chicago, 1935

Towns, Elmer L. Editor, A History of Religious Educators, Baker Book House, Grand Rapids, MI, 1975

Transworldradio, Magazine published by TWR., 300 Gregson Drive, Cary, NC 27512

Trueblood, Elton, The Company of the Committed, Harper and Row, New York, 1961

Trueblood, Elton, The Incendiary Fellowship, Harper and Row, New York, 1967

TWR Prayer Request list, Published quarterly by TWR.

TWR Web site, www.gospelcom.net/twr

United Bible Societies Web site, www.biblesociety.org/

Urbana Web site: www.urbana.org

U.S. News and World Report, U.S. News and World Report, Inc., New York, 1996

Ward, Kaari, Ed., JESUS And His Times, The Reader's Digest Association, Inc., Pleasantville, New York, 1987

Wieruszowski, Helene, The Medieval University, D.Van Nostrand Company, Inc, Princeton, NJ, 1966

World Vision Today, World Vision, Inc. Tacoma, WA 98481

Wycliffe Bible Translators' Web site: www.wycliffe.org

Suggested Reading

Foakes Jackson, F. J., *History of the Christian Church to A.D 461, 1914*

Gordon, C. H, *The Living Past, 1941*

Gordon, C. H., *Adventures in the Near East, 1957,*

Gordon, C. H., *Before the Bible, 1962*

Hamilton, Edith, *Witness to the Truth.*

Hunter, A. M., *Interpreting the Parables, 1960*

Ingham, Kenneth, *Reformers in India, 1793 to 1833 An Account of the Work of Christian Missionaries on Behalf of Social Reform, Cambridge, 1956*

Jeremias, Joachim, *The Parables of Jesus, 1947*

Ladd, George Edon, *The Gospel of the Kingdom, 1959*

Ladd, George Edon, *The Presence of the Future, 1974*

Latourette, K.S., *History of the Expansion of Christianity, Vol. I (1938), Vol. II (1939)*

Loukes, Harold, *The Castle and the Field, George Allen and Unwin, London, 1959*

Nicolai, Philipp, *The Reign of Christ, 1956*

Oliver, Roland, *The Missionary Factor in East Africa, London and New York, 1952*

Rauschenbush, *Christianity and the Social Gospel, 1907*

Rauschenbush, *Theology of Social Gospel, 1917*

Ridderbos, Herman, *The Coming of the Kingdom, 1950*

Sine, Tom, *The Mustard Seed Conspiracy*

Stoll, David, *Is Latin America Turning Protestant?*

Stott, *Involvement; Being a Responsible Christian in a Non Christian Society*, Revell, Old Tappan, NJ., 1985

Trueblood, *The Yoke of Christ.*

Willems, Emilio, *Followers of the New Faith*, 1967

Wright, G.E., *The O.T. Against Its Environment*, 1950

ENDNOTES

1 *Hymns of the Living Faith, (Winona Lake,IN,1951) p.512*

2 *G. W. Griffith, The Divine Program,(Chicago,1923), p.54*

3 *R.K.Harrison, Old Testament Times, (Grand Rapids,1970) p.225*

4 *ibid*

5 *E.W.Heaton, Everyday Life in Old Testament Times,(New York,1956)p.63*

6 *Roy Porter, The Greatest Benefit to Mankind, (New York, London, 1997)p.23*

7 *ibid*

8 *Heaton, op.cit. p.71*

9 *Madeleine S. Miller and J. Lane Miller, Harper's Encyclopedia of Bible Life, (San Francisco, 1978),p.37*

10 *ibid, p.36*

11 *Porter, op.cit. p.15*

12 *ibid, p.19*

13 *2Chr.6:28,Ps.91:6,Rev. 21:9*

14 *ibid, p.23*

15 *Carole Rawcliffe, Medicine and Society in Later Medieval England, (Phoenix Mill, England, 1995), p.3*

16 *ibid*

17 *Porter, op.cit. p.124*

18 *Heaton, op.cit. p.195*

19 *Rawcilffe, op.cit. p.9*

20 *ibid*

21 *Miller and Miller, op.cit. p.240*

[22] *Heaton, op.cit. p.160*

[23] *ibid, p.169*

[24] *Francis A.Schaeffer, How Should We Then Live?,(Old Tappan, NJ, 1976), p.21*

[25] *Edith Hamilton, The Roman Way,(New York, 1932), p.194*

[26] *ibid*

[27] *Heaton, op.cit. p.141*

[28] *William Barclay, The Letters to the Galatians and Ephesians, (Philadelphia,1958), p.212*

[29] *Mazzolan, Lidia, Storoni, Empire Without End,(New York and London,1976), p. xxix*

[30] *Edith Hamilton, The Greek Way,(New York, 1930), p.160*

[31] *ibid, p.186*

[32] *Mazzolan et al., op.cit. p.xxix*

[33] *Hamilton, The Greek Way, op.cit. p. 174*

[34] *Barclay, op.cit. p.214*

[35] *Harrison, op.cit. p.12*

[36] *See 1 Kings 5:13–18;9:15–23*

[37] *Heaton, op.cit. p.141*

[38] *Miller and Miller, op.cit. p.232*

[39] *Henry Snyder Gehman, Ed., The New Westminster Dictionary of the Bible, (Philadelphia, 1970), p.82*

[40] *Heaton, op.cit. p.68*

[41] *ibid*

[42] *Barclay, op.cit. p.199*

[43] *ibid, p.201*

[44] *Barclay, op.cit. p.201*

[45] *ibid*

[46] *ibid, p.202*

[47] *Hamilton, The Roman Way, op.cit. p.248*

[48] *Barclay, op.cit. p.208*

[49] *ibid, p.209*

[50] *ibid, p.208*

[51] *Rawcliffe, op.cit. p.4*

[52] *Heaton, op.cit. p.79*

[53] *Ralph Gower, The Lion Encyclopedia of the Bible, Pat Alexander, ED. (The Reader's Digest Association, Inc., Pleasantville, NY with permission of Lion Publishing Corporation, Batavia, IL,1987), p.162*

[54] *ibid, p. 161*

[55] *Kaari Ward, Ed., JESUS And His Times, (The Reader's Digest Association, Inc., Pleasantville, NY, Montreal, 1987), p.151*

[56] *ibid, p.152*

[57] *ibid, p.159*

[58] *ibid*

[59] *Ralph Gower, op.cit. p.246*

[60] *David Clines, The Lion Encyclopedia of the Bible, Pat Alexander, ED. (The Reader's Digest Association, Inc., Pleasantville, NY with permission of Lion Publishing Corporation, Batavia, IL,1987),p.135*

[61] *Kaari Ward, op.cit. p.156*

[62] *Alfred Edersheim, The Life And Times Of Jesus The Messiah, Longmans, Green, and Co., New York, 1906), Vol I., p.230*

[63] *Michael Grant, The History of Ancient Israel,(New York, 1984)*

[64] *Richard E. Gross, Heritage of American Education, (Boston, 1962), p.33*

[65] *ibid*

[66] *ibid, p.37*

[67] *Mazollan et al., op.cit. p.xxx*

[68] *ibid, p.34*

[69] *Leonard Hayflick, Discover, VOL.23, NO 12. Buena Vista Magazines,(New York), p.15*

[70] *Jaroslav Pelikan, Jesus Through The Centuries, (New Haven and London, 1985), p.1*

[71] *ibid, p.2*

[72] *ibid, p.25*

[73] *ibid, p.32*

[74] *Daniel J. Boorstin, Hidden History, (New York,1987), p. 309*

[75] *Alice Galvin, Ed., American Catholic Higher Education, (Notre Dame, IN, 1992), p.131*

[76] *L. J. Daly, The Medieval University,(New York,1961), p.4*

[77] *ibid, p.1*

[78] *Elmer L. Towns, Ed., A History of Religious Educators, (Grand Rapids,1975), p.14*

[79] *ibid*

[80] *Daly, op.cit. p.7*

[81] *Tim Dowley, Ed., The History of Christianity, (Oxford, 1977) pp. 283–284*

[82] *Daly, op.cit. p.xiii*

[83] *Dowley, op.cit. p.286*

[84] *Towns, op. cit. p.101*

85 *ibid, p.102*

86 *ibid, p.104*

87 *ibid, p.106*

88 *ibid, p.115*

89 *ibid*

90 *ibid, p.169*

91 *ibid*

92 *ibid, p.212*

93 *Boorstin, op.cit. p.72*

94 *Schaeffer, op.cit. p.132*

95 *ibid, pp.132–133*

96 *ibid*

97 *ibid, p.131*

98 *Dowley, op.cit. p.48*

99 *ibid*

100 *ibid, p.49*

101 *The following are only a few of the many colleges and universities started by missionaries: India: Serampore College (1819) Wilson College in Bombay (1832) Madras Christian College (1837) United Theological College at Bangalore (1901); China: Thirty three Christian institutions by 1913 including Peking, Yenching, and St. John's Universities; Japan: Doshisha University (1874); Beirut: The American University; Constantinople: Robert College (1860); Africa: Fourah Baby College in Sierra Leone (1827) Lovedale Institute in Cape Colony (1841); (Clouse et.al. 1993 p. 503)*

102 *Albert Lyons, R. Joseph Petrucelli II, MEDICINE, An Illustrated History, (New York, 1978), p.265*

[103] *Gross, op.cit. p.59*

[104] *Lyons, op.cit. p.119*

[105] *Porter, op.cit. p.87*

[106] *ibid,*

[107] *ibid, p.195*

[108] *ibid, p.235*

[109] *Barclay, op.cit. p.209*

[110] *Lyons, op.cit. p.265*

[111] *Porter, op.cit. p.87*

[112] *ibid, p.272*

[113] *ibid. p.111*

[114] *ibid*

[115] *Lyons, op.cit. p.544*

[116] *Porter, op.cit. p.111*

[117] *Lyons, p.283*

[118] *Porter, op.cit. p.110*

[119] *ibid, p.71*

[120] *ibid, p.88*

[121] *ibid, p.112*

[122] *ibid, p.110*

[123] *ibid*

[124] *ibid, p.113*

[125] *Irvine Louden, Ed., Western Medicine, (Oxford, 1997), p.58*

[126] *ibid, p.63*

[127] *ibid, p.485*

[128] *ibid, p.544*

[129] *Lyons, p.345*

[130] *ibid*

[131] *As recent as 1961 Elton Trueblood wrote that the Church needs to make a frank recognition of its own "relative failure" and that it is in "retreat".(Trueblood, The Company of the Committed. 1961 p.2.)*

[132] *John Bright, The Kingdom of God,(Nashville, 1953), p.218*

[133] *Robert G. Clouse, Richard V. Pierard, Edwin M. Yamauchi, Two Kingdoms, (Chicago,1993), p.503*

[134] *Tara E. Sheets, Ed., Encyclopedia of Associations, (Farmington Hills, MI, 1999), pp. 17, 884–18, 024*

[135] *Charles Colson, The Body, (Dallas, 1992), p.199*

[136] *Except where other wise noted, information about Campus Crusade for Christ International has been gathered from its Website, www.ccci.org.*

[137] *Campus Crusade For Christ, Inc, 2001 Annual Report, (Orlando, 2001), p.2*

[138] *Information about FamilyLife is taken from its Web site, familylife.com/about/who_we_are.asp,5/03/03*

[139] *Annual Report, op.cit. pp.3–4*

[140] *ibid, p.4*

[141] *Unless otherwise noted information about World Vision was taken from its web site, worldvision.org, 3/27/00 and its magazine World Vision Today, (Tacoma, WA) and its various publications. Used with permission*

[142] *Except where other wise noted, information about Prison Fellowship International has been gathered from its Website,* www.pfi.org/international.htm, *4/22/03, 5/03/03*

[143] *Except where other wise noted, information about Trans*

World Radio has been gathered from its Website www.
gospelcom.net/twr and is used by permission.

[144] Transworldradio, (Cary, NC),Feb. 2003, p.24

[145] ibid, Feb. 2003, p.3

[146] ibid, p.6

[147] ibid, Nov. 2002, p.45

[148] ibid, Nov. 2002, p.10

[149] ibid, p.20

[150] ibid, p.1

[151] All information about Intervarsity Christian Fellowship reported here has been gained from its website www. intervarsity.org 4/30/03 Used by permission.

[152] ibid.

[153] All information about the Urbana Student Missions Conference is taken from its Web page, www.urbana.org 4/30/03,and is used by permission.

[154] All information about UBS reported here was gained from its website www.biblesociety.org/ 5/03/03

[155] All information about Wycliffe Bible Translators and Summer Institute of Linguistics, not otherwise cited, reported here has been gained from Wycliffe's website www.wycliffe.org 4/30/03 & 5/09/03 and used by permission.

[156] information about JAARS reported here has been gained from JAARS' website www.jaars.org 5/09/03 and is used by permission.

[157] In Focus, (Orlando, 2004), p.1

[158] Intercessor, (Orlando, March 2004), p.1

[159] All information about CCCU reported here has been

gained from its website www.CCCU.org. *5/09/03 Used by permission.*

160 *Roberts Today,(Rochester, NY, Summer 2004), p.13*

161 *Information in this section has been excerpted from the Focus on the Family web site* www.family.org *5/15/03 Copyright© 2004 Focus on the Family. All rights reserved. International copyright secured. Used by permission.*

162 *All information about Promise Keepers reported here has been gained from its website, promisekeepers. org5/03/03*

163 *ibid.*

164 *30 Days Muslim Prayer Focus,(Colorado Springs, 2001), p.2*

165 *ibid, p.3*

166 *ibid, p.1*

167 *Fund raising letter, Nov. 24,2004*

168 *Campus Crusade for Christ, Ministry Highlights,(Orlando, Dec. 2004)*

169 *Campus Crusade for Christ, Today, Orlando, Dec. 2004), p.1*

170 *ibid*

171 *All the information presented in this section, including the quotations, was taken from the Home Schooling Web site www.findartices.com/cf_dis_g 5/15/03*

172 *ibid.*

173 *ibid.*

174 *Prayerline,(Waxhaw, NC, Dec.Jan., 2005), p.4*

175 *Modern Reformation, (Philadelphia, 2000), Vol.9 #2, p.10*

[176] *wyclife.org/wbt-usa/report/letter2002.htm, 4/30/03. Used by permission.*

[177] *Casa Grande Dispatch, (Casa Grande, AZ Nov. 18,2004), p.4*

[178] *Beyond,(Orlando, Fall 2004), p.3*

[179] *ibid, p.9*

[180] *Wycliffe.org, op.cit. 4/30/03*

[181] *The Pilgrim Hymnal, The Pilgrim Press, (Boston and Chicago,1935), p.373*

[182] *Pilgrim Hymnal, Op.cit. p.3*

[183] *italics mine*

[184] *Schaeffer, op.cit. p.119*

[185] *David Chidester, Christianity, A Global History,(San Francisco, 2000), p. 537*

[186] *ibid*

[187] *Bright, op.cit. p. 218*

[188] *Elton Trueblood, The Company of the Committed,(New York, 1961), p.101*

[189] *John Stott, The Contemporary Christian, (Downers Grove, IL, 1992), p. 334*

[190] *Stott, op.cit. p.326*

[191] *ibid, p.327*

[192] *Matthew Henry, COMMENTARY ON THE WHOLE BIBLE, (Grand Rapids, 1961), p.169*

[193] *ibid, p.91*

[194] *Henry, op.cit. p.183*

[195] *ibid, p.208*

[196] *Bright, op.cit. p.212*

[197] *Henry, op.cit. p.671*

[198] *Bright p.215*

[199] *ibid, p.216*

[200] *Robert Jamieson, A.R. Faussett, David Brown, David, Commentary, Critical and Explanatory on the Whole Bible, (Grand Rapids,no date given),p.380*

[201] *Henry, op.cit. p.720*

[202] *John H. Stek, The NIV Bible, (Grand Rapids, 1995), p.1102*

[203] *Henry, op.cit. p.648*

[204] *Henry, op.cit. p.682*

[205] *Stott, op.cit. p.351*

[206] *ibid, p.375*

[207] *Bright, op.cit. p.244*

[208] *G. G. D. Kilpatrick, The Interpreter's Bible, Vol.V, (New York,1953), p.250*

[209] *ibid, p.180*

[210] *ibid*

[211] *Bright, op.cit. p.248*

[212] *R. B. Y. Scott, Interpreter's Bible, Vol.V, op.cit. p.345*

[213] *Henry Sloane Coffin, Interpreter's Bible, Vol.V, op.cit. p.577*

[214] *Shirley C. Guthrie, Jr., Christian Doctrine,(Richmond, VA,1968), p.279*

[215] *ibid*

[216] *Henry, op.cit. p.1104*

[217] *George A. Buttrick, Interpreter's Bible, Vol. VII, p.452*

[218] *ibid, p.622*

[219] *Steven R. Donziger, Ed., The Real World on Crime,(New York, 1996), p.66*

[220] U.S. News and World Report, Dec. 16, 1996,Volume 121 No. 24, p.32

[221] Trueblood, 1967, op.cit. p.25

[222] Richard Collier,The General Next to God, (Collins, 1965) pp.104–109

[223] Stott, op.cit. p.362

[224] Griffith, op.cit. p.99

[225] Trueblood, 1967, op.cit. p.18

[226] Perry C. Cotham, *Politics, Americanism, and Christianity,* (Grand Rapids, 1976), p.240

[227] Charles Colson, *Kingdoms in Conflict,* (Grand Rapids, 1987), p.84

[228] ibid, p.46

[229] See, Alistiar Cooke's, *Alistiar Cooke's America,* (New York, 1973), for an excellent discussion of this attempt.

[230] Cotham, op.cit. p.235

[231] William J. Bouwsma, *The Waning of the Renaissance 1550–1640,* (New Haven, 2000), p.ix

[232] Schaeffer, op.cit. p.85

[233] Clouse et.al, op.cit. p.487

[234] Stott, op.cit. p.351

[235] ibid

[236] Clouse et.al., op.cit. p.477

[237] Clouse et.al., op.cit. p.476

[238] ibid

[239] ibid, p.494

240 ibid

241 ibid

242 ibid

243 ibid

244 Pelican, op.cit. p.217

245 ibid

246 ibid

ABOUT THE AUTHOR

Grove and Charity Armstrong
Photo by Mary Lou Lawton, Elizabethtown, PA.

Grove Armstrong, a graduate of Roberts Wesleyan College and Asbury Theological Seminary, served thirty-three years in the pastoral ministry. From 1956 to 1973, he ministered in Free Methodist Churches in Pennsylvania and New Jersey and from 1980 until 1996 was Senior Minister of the Central Congregational Church in Derry, New Hampshire. He served on the Congregational Foundation for Theological Studies and in 1992 was awarded the Dr. Harry R. Butman Award for Outstanding Service to the National Association of Congregational Christian Churches for his work in writing the Lay Minister's Training Course. From 1974 to 1980, he was a debit agent with the Prudential Insurance Company in Flanders, NJ, where he won several awards for sales achievements. Throughout his ministry, he wrote for newspapers, denominational magazines, devotional booklets, and *The International Sunday School Lessons.* He self-published *The Art of Personal Worship,* which has gone through five editions. Presently he is a seminar instructor with Prison Fellowship and ministers regularly in the Arizona State Prison system. He plays in a senior softball league and sings baritone with a barbershop chorus. Grove and his wife, Charity, currently winter in Case Grande, Arizona, and in the summer travel in a motor home. They have assisted in the construction of four homes with Habitat for Humanity and volunteer at Camp Susque, a Christian summer camp. Of their eight children, three are teachers, two engineers, two lawyers, and one a nurse. They thank God for their twenty-four grandchildren and four great-grandchildren.

All the profits from the sale of this book are dedicated to missions, some of which are mentioned in this book. Missionaries or Mission Organizations who would like to use this book to increase funding for their work are encouraged to contact the author at groveandcharity@juno.com for information.

Contact Grove Armstrong
groveandcharity@juno.com
or order more copies of this book at

TATE PUBLISHING, LLC

127 East Trade Center Terrace
Mustang, Oklahoma 73064

(888) 361 - 9473

Tate Publishing, LLC

www.tatepublishing.com